W9-CHI-273

THE LIBRARY OF AFRICAN-AMERICAN BIOGRAPHY

John David Smith, editor

Booker T. Washington

Booker T. Washington

BLACK LEADERSHIP IN
THE AGE OF JIM CROW

Raymond W. Smock

*The Library of
African-American Biography*

IVAN R. DEE · CHICAGO

BOOKER T. WASHINGTON. Copyright © 2009 by Raymond W. Smock. All rights reserved, including the right to reproduce this book or portions thereof in any form. For information, address: Ivan R. Dee, Publisher, 1332 North Halsted Street, Chicago 60642, a member of the Rowman & Littlefield Publishing Group. Manufactured in the United States of America and printed on acid-free paper.

www.ivanrdee.com

The paperback edition of this book carries the ISBN 978-1-56663-866-1.

Library of Congress Cataloging-in-Publication Data:
Smock, Raymond.
   Booker T. Washington : black leadership in the age of Jim Crow / Raymond W. Smock.
      p. cm.
   Includes bibliographical references and index.
   ISBN 978-1-56663-725-1 (cloth : acid-free paper)
   1. Washington, Booker T., 1856–1915. 2. African Americans— Biography. 3. Educators—United States—Biography. I. Title.
E185.97.W4S667 2009
370.92—dc22
   [B]   2009003277

For Phyllis

Contents

Acknowledgments

JOHN DAVID SMITH encouraged me to write this book, and I am grateful to him for the chance to return to my earlier scholarly interest, when I spent almost two decades sifting through Washington's private correspondence as co-editor of the *Booker T. Washington Papers*. It has been a great pleasure to work with Ivan Dee, a truly masterful editor, who worked diligently to make this a better book. I also benefited from an early reading of the manuscript by Elaine Rendler-McQueeney of George Mason University.

My greatest debts, however, are older ones to friends and colleagues of long standing who had nothing to do with this particular book but everything to do with my understanding of Booker T. Washington. Foremost among them is my mentor and longtime friend and colleague on the Booker T. Washington Papers, Louis R. Harlan, the preeminent scholar of Washington's life and career. It was a rare privilege and a great joy to work with Louis Harlan for so many years. The late August Meier first introduced me to Booker T. Washington when I was an undergraduate at Roosevelt University in Chicago. His book *Negro Thought in America* had just been published, and I was in his first class to use this volume to study Washington's career. Pete Daniel, a fellow student of Louis Harlan's in the 1960s, was writing his pioneering study of peonage, and we spent many hours together working through the racial thicket of the late nineteenth and early twentieth centuries.

Avon Kirkland, an exemplary documentary filmmaker in Berkeley, California, and I have had coast-to-coast telephone marathons over the past several years discussing Booker. T. Washington and sharing ideas for Kirkland's documentary film on Washington's career. I also want to thank Kat Covell, co-producer of the Booker T. Washington documentary project at New Images Productions, for her assistance with the photographs used in this book.

My thanks to the staff of the Shepherd University Library in Shepherdstown, West Virginia, for their help in locating volumes on Booker T. Washington.

Any obligatory reference to my wife, Phyllis, would be totally inadequate to express the complete support and constant encouragement she has given me for almost a half-century.

R. W. S.

Shepherdstown, West Virginia
March 2009

Booker T. Washington

Booker T. Washington in History and Memory

꧁ Booker T. Washington was the most prominent black educator, race leader, and international celebrity of the late nineteenth and early twentieth centuries. Yet his career was shrouded in controversy from the moment he assumed the mantle of the leading spokesman for his race following his electrifying speech before the Cotton States and International Exposition in Atlanta, Georgia, in September 1895. There he offered the South, and the nation, a plan to settle the rapidly deteriorating conditions experienced by black Americans during a time that one historian called the "nadir of Negro life in America."

Washington's plan called for blacks to be given the opportunity to advance through education and training in basic trades so they could advance economically. This would help move millions of poor blacks just a generation from slavery into positions to become productive and respected citizens. It would be a ticket to upward mobility, personal freedom, success, and, most important, acceptance as full citizens.

To gain this foothold on the economic ladder, Washington made a bargain with the white South, most of whose politicians espoused white supremacy. He promised that blacks would not agitate for civil and political rights or push for social equality in the South. He would bow to the reality of Jim

Crow practices, bargain for time to make his plan work, and hope that racial conditions would improve as blacks proved their ability to make economic and educational progress.

Washington's program, later called the Atlanta Compromise by his critics, was both ingenious and deeply flawed. He would spend the rest of his life trying to make the bargain of his Atlanta Address work to improve the fortunes of blacks. It was the single most important speech he ever delivered, and it defined his role as a race leader. But even at his great moment of triumph in Atlanta, where he distilled his plan for the future of his race into a remarkable eight-minute talk, he built himself a trap from which he never escaped. White supremacists embraced Washington's plan because it accommodated to the prevailing sentiment that blacks were not socially or politically equal to whites. Washington's black critics, who were intrigued by the Atlanta Address at first, quickly determined that Washington had bargained away too much for a racial peace that never materialized.

Time and circumstances have reduced the memory of Washington's role in American history to a faded stereotype in the public consciousness, even while professional historians and educators still write about him and consider him a major figure in the story of America. Each generation of Americans has viewed him through eyes shaped by its own times. He has been hero as well as villain. In his own lifetime he was called a Moses, one who would lead blacks from bondage to freedom. He was also called a lackey of his white supporters, the wealthy industrialists who helped fund his program. A half-century after his death he was all but forgotten. During the civil rights movement of the 1960s he was called an "Uncle Tom"—a slave loyal to his white masters. In either mode, as hero or villain, as Moses or Uncle Tom, his story is an essential part of American history and black history.

In December 2006 the *Atlantic Monthly* published the results of a survey and compiled a list of the one hundred most influential figures in American history. Booker T. Washington made the list: "an educator and a champion of self-help, he tried to lead black Americans up from slavery." Only seven other black Americans could be found on the list, including the civil rights leader Martin Luther King, Jr.; the baseball player Jackie Robinson, who broke the major league color line; the intellectual W. E. B. Du Bois; the abolitionist Frederick Douglass; the jazz musician Louis Armstrong; the jurist Thurgood Marshall; and the slave insurrectionist Nat Turner.

As we enter what some historians have called the "post–civil rights era," Washington's race leadership has increasingly become the subject of new articles, symposia, and biographies. His name is again on the lips of social commentators who suggest that Barack Obama and Booker T. Washington share some qualities and styles of leadership, albeit from vastly different times and circumstances. Both Washington and Obama are described as conciliators and bargainers who play down the troubled racial past of the nation, look for compromise with whites, and promise a brighter future.

In his book *A Bound Man* (2007), the conservative black writer Shelby Steele offers penetrating observations about black leadership styles from Frederick Douglass to Barack Obama. Steele posits two major types of black leadership: bargainers and challengers. The abolitionist Frederick Douglass challenged the slave system with moral outrage. Booker T. Washington bargained with white power for time and opportunity to advance. The civil rights movement returned to a challenge mode. Now, in a post–civil rights era, the first black president of the United States ran a campaign that did not raise old racial wounds to gain advantage with some voters at the risk of losing others.

This biography presents Washington essentially as a bargainer, a compromiser, and a conciliator because these terms describe his public face and his public utterances on racial issues. Behind his public face, however, Washington found ways to challenge Jim Crow. He developed an underground attack against racial injustice. Thus he might be called both a bargainer and a challenger. But the labels alone are insufficient without understanding the historical context and the particular circumstances of his actions. Washington could be effective in either mode, but the thrust of his career and the best gauge to his leadership remains his public stance and his role as a spokesman and a celebrity who affected his generation, both blacks and whites, like no other.

The historic fact that an American of African descent has been elected president of the United States simply could not have happened in Booker Washington's time, in Jim Crow America, where racial discrimination, segregation, and disfranchisement were so blatantly oppressive. Senator John McCain suggested as much in his concession speech in 2008 when he said, "America today is a world away from the cruel and frightful bigotry of [Washington's] time." In Jim Crow America white politicians openly ran campaigns that called for the preservation of white supremacy, with blacks "in their place" as second-class citizens. It was a time when state constitutions were rewritten to disfranchise blacks and laws passed to prevent racial intermarriage. The word "miscegenation," or race mixing, was something to be feared and shunned. In such an atmosphere Booker T. Washington found himself severely limited in what he could say and do publicly by the dominant and virulent anti-black sentiment that surrounded him and ultimately controlled him.

The question pondered by Washington and other race leaders of his time is still a relevant one in the beginning decade of the twenty-first century: Will the time come when the United States, and the rest of the world, will be free of racism and ethnic hatreds that deny blacks and other minorities their right to live free and equal? As long as this question remains unanswered, the story of Washington's leadership will be instructive. And if the day comes when race and ethnicity play little or no role in the politics and culture of the nation or the world, Washington's story will remain as a stark reminder of the cost of our racially segregated past.

Washington could never speak for white America, even though he had many white allies. He believed he represented the "best" thinking among people of his own race and that of the white race. His definition of "best" meant those whites who would not oppose black economic advancement and who would not be motivated by hatred of his race. The "best" blacks, in Washington's mind, were the sensible members of his race who would work hard to get an education, live quiet and productive lives, and find honorable ways to accommodate to the prevailing racism around them without agitating for their rights and causing trouble. His was a waiting game—waiting for the day when prejudice and hatred would diminish to the point that it would no longer impede advancement.

On October 17, 1901, Booker T. Washington went to the White House to have dinner with President Theodore Roosevelt. Washington was at the height of his power and influence: he went to discuss Republican party politics in the South. Roosevelt sought Washington's advice because no one had a better grasp of Republican issues among Southern blacks. When word got out that a black man, even the noted educator Booker T. Washington, had dined with the president and his family—in the White House—it prompted an outburst of criticism in the South. Washington, despite his prominence, had crossed the color line. Because of his skin color he had no business dining and socializing with whites, especially with the president and his family. Such behavior suggested he was the social equal of any white man. Such were the strictures of Jim Crow America.

The America that Washington lived in was a totalitarian system when it came to matters of race. The great majority of the ten million blacks who lived in the United States at the turn of the twentieth century, no matter what their walk of life, their education level, their economic status, or their geographical location, were never free of Jim Crow segregation and discrimination.

The Jim Crow era arose in the years during and after Reconstruction in an uneven pattern throughout the Southern states and eventually spread into the North. Jim Crow, a name derived from a white minstrel-show actor in the 1830s, received official sanction from the Supreme Court in the famous 1896 *Plessy* v. *Ferguson* decision, which gave constitutional approval to the segregation of the races in public transportation and in schools. More than fifty years later the Court overturned the *Plessy* decision in *Brown* v. *Board of Education* (1954), holding that separate schools for blacks and whites were inherently unequal and that racial segregation had denied political rights and created a second-class status for black Americans. It took another decade, and a massive civil rights movement, before Congress passed the landmark Civil Rights Act of 1964. The Jim Crow system of racial segregation was finally overturned, but it died slow and hard—it would be easy to demonstrate that de facto Jim Crow still exists in too many areas of American life. In February 2008 the United States Congress, for the first time in history, passed a resolution of apology for slavery and Jim Crow. The resolution acknowledges that "African-Americans continue to suffer from the consequences of slavery and Jim Crow . . ."

The noteworthy White House dinner was depicted in a lithograph by C. H. Thomas and P. H. Lacey in 1903. The actual dinner included Roosevelt's family. *(Smithsonian Institution)*

Booker T. Washington was one of a few black Americans who penetrated the consciousness of whites in America. A century ago, if whites were asked who was the most famous black person in America, they would likely have named him. Or, if they were inclined toward sports, they might have named the sensational boxer Jack Johnson. White newspapers seldom covered black news unless it involved a crime or a sporting event. Washington was the exception. He remained popular in the minds of many Americans, black and white, long after his death. He had mass appeal and was a popular speaker who appeared on stage with the luminaries of his day, including Mark Twain.

But Washington's personal popularity alone was never enough to stem the tide of violent racism and bigotry that was all around him. Just three years after his death, black American soldiers who fought to make the world safe for democracy in World War I returned home changed men. They had seen parts of the world that did not treat black men the same way they were treated in America. They were welcomed as heroes in France, only to return to racially segregated America, where some of them were actually lynched while still wearing their uniforms. The old way, Booker T. Washington's way, of accommodating to white America, did not seem to be working. Turning the other cheek in the hope of achieving racial advancement had failed.

Race leadership after Washington's time passed to talented and dedicated men like James Weldon Johnson and Walter White, who worked through organizations like the NAACP, founded in 1909, just six years before Washington's death. The intellectual leadership of the race shifted to Du Bois, who did his best work within the NAACP. Du Bois, however, would never be the national celebrity, especially among whites, that Washington had been. His acerbic personality and academic pretensions did not endear him to large numbers of blacks, who were more likely to be moved by his ideas than his actual presence. Today Du Bois ranks as a great man of ideas who championed full civil rights and equality for black Americans. His penetrating critique of Washington's leadership remains the gold standard when considering the limits of Washington's role as a race leader.

It took a new generation of leaders and numerous organizations with a variety of voices, including the intriguing Malcolm X, the Student Non-Violent Coordinating Committee (SNCC), the Congress of Racial Equality (CORE), the Black Panthers, and the Black Power movement led by Stokely Carmichael and others to beat down Jim Crow. But it was Martin Luther King, Jr., who captured the vital center of the civil rights movement and gained a large following of blacks and whites.

The Jim Crow era that began as Booker T. Washington came of age did not end for another half-century after his death. Those who fought openly against racial injustice are easier to see as heroes than someone like Washington, who accommodated to Jim Crow and tried to find ways to advance his race from within that closed system. His legacy in the second half of the twentieth century and into our own time is burdened by what appears to be unheroic, overly cautious behavior. Admiration for his role as an important educator has not diminished; even his harshest critics conceded that Washington's founding of Tuskegee Institute and his role as a promoter of black education and racial self-help were noble pursuits. But the race leader who espoused gradual advancement and accommodation to white power came under the harshest attack.

Twenty-five years after Washington's death, in 1940, his image was dusted off and shaped for a new generation in need of a black hero. Faced with the racist propaganda of Nazi Germany, with its theories of Aryan superiority, the United States countered with a program to recognize black contributions to American life and culture. When the Post Office issued a series of commemorative stamps featuring famous Americans, Booker T. Washington's image appeared in the educator series. He was the only black American included in any category—it was the first time the image of a black person had graced a U.S. postage stamp.

During World War II a Liberty ship, one of the vessels that ferried troops to Europe and Asia, was named for Booker T. Washington. It was christened with much fanfare by the great black singer Marian Anderson as part of the effort to promote better race relations in time of war. Just a year before, Anderson had been Jim-Crowed by the Daughters of the American Revolution, who refused her the use of their Constitution Hall in Washington, D.C., for a concert. Eleanor Roosevelt, wife of the president, arranged for Anderson to give her concert outdoors on the steps of the Lincoln Memorial. Seventy-five thousand people attended.

After World War II the United States and the Soviet Union engaged in a complex and lengthy cold war, complete with massive propaganda campaigns on both sides. Criticizing American race relations, the Soviets asked how the United States could boast of democracy and freedom when millions of black Americans were denied equal rights under the law and suffered daily from racial discrimination in public transportation, schools, housing, and opportunities to advance to full citizenship.

Within this cold war context, Booker T. Washington's story again became a positive American symbol in the international propaganda war. Washington's image reappeared in 1946, this time as a role model of success and upward mobility, on a commemorative half-dollar issued by the U.S. Mint—the first time a U.S. coin had featured the image of a black person. While his profile appeared on the obverse of the coin, the real message of his life and the message the government wanted the world to see, was on the reverse side, which showed a humble slave cabin with the motto: "From Slave Cabin to Hall of Fame." The Washington commemorative coin had the longest run of any coin of its type in American history. In 1952 the Mint issued a second coin with Washington's image joined in a dual profile with the black agricultural scientist George Washington Carver, whom Washington had hired to teach at Tuskegee Institute in 1897. Minted at the height of anti-Communist hysteria, the coin featured the legend "Americanism." On the hundredth anniversary of Washington's birth a commemorative stamp depicted a log cabin similar to the one in which Washington was born.

The intellectual ferment of the 1960s included numerous assaults on big government and big business. Radicals believed that the "Establishment" needed to change before America could change for the better. Nineteenth-century captains of industry, even those who were noted philanthropists, were often blamed for society's ills. Booker T. Washington was painted with the same brush. Even though he was a former slave who had risen through his own efforts, he was now linked with Andrew Carnegie and John D. Rockefeller as part of the despised Establishment. This former slave had somehow achieved a status as part of "elite" America.

In 1963 the historian August Meier published his seminal work *Negro Thought in America, 1880–1915,* which began a reevaluation of Washington's leadership even while many activists in the civil rights movement were dismantling his reputation. Meier portrayed Washington as "surreptitiously engaged in undermining the American race system by a direct attack upon disfranchisement and segregation . . . in spite of his strictures against political activity he was a powerful politician in his own right."

Louis Harlan's later biography of Washington, based upon extensive use of his private papers, painted a far more complex picture of Washington's character and the inner workings of his role as a race leader than had existed. Washington's papers revealed an intriguing "secret life," as Harlan called it, an inside view of how Washington operated and how he secretly fought against Jim Crow and his black critics. For the first time in such detail, Harlan was able to look behind Washington's public mask. While his public persona often took on the appearance of a meek rabbit, secretly he could be a shrewd fox and an able politician. After

Harlan's biography it was impossible to return to earlier views of Washington or to accept at face value the view of himself put forward in his own autobiography, composed as the American success story of a humble slave who worked hard, got an education, and rose to fame.

By the 1980s and 1990s Washington's story and his race leadership prompted a new reinterpretation at the hands of conservative thinkers, both black and white. They rediscovered Washington as a prominent Republican from an earlier time. As the nation debated ways to address racial issues with programs like affirmative action, in which the government mandated hiring quotas to offset racial discrimination, many conservatives saw Washington as a model of self-help and individual initiative that required no government intervention. Washington, in this new interpretation, was someone who would not expect the government to fix racial inequities. Although affirmative action did not exist in Washington's time, some conservatives found little trouble casting him as someone who would have opposed it. Almost a century after his death, Washington continues to be part of the dialogue on race, sometimes twisted and turned to fit new circumstances.

If Washington had not been a powerful presence in the history of the black experience in America, he would by now have faded into distant memory. But he keeps returning to haunt some and inspire others. A good part of the difficulty in studying Washington's life rests in the troubled times in which he lived. The failures of Reconstruction and the repression of Jim Crow are parts of American history that cut against the grain of the great American success story, both in myth and reality. They challenge the mythology of continually expanding American freedom.

Washington's ultimate failure to stem the tide of Jim Crow racism came from his inability to recognize how deep and powerful racial prejudice was in America. He hoped the example of his personal success story could be duplicated in some degree by millions of others. Certainly his quest for an education put him on the road to salvation and freedom, just as it did for countless other newly freed slaves. But he never fully grasped how unique he was as an example of black success in America.

CHAPTER ONE

The Quest for Freedom

So from an old clay cabin in Virginia's hills, Booker T. Washington rose up to be one of the nation's great leaders. He lit a torch in Alabama, then darkness fled.—Martin Luther King, Jr.

My owner's name was James Burroughs, and I am quite sure he was above the average in the treatment of his slaves. That is, except for a few cases they were not cruelly whipped.—Booker T. Washington, *The Story of My Life and Work*, 1900

He was born with intense grey eyes and a light skin color, the property of a farmer in Franklin County, Virginia, in 1856. He never knew his white father, possibly one of the young men from a nearby farm. In his entire life he never learned anything about his ancestors other than his mother, Jane. He spent the first nine years of his life in a one-room log cabin, about fourteen by sixteen feet, with a clay floor. He lived with his mother, his younger half-sister Amanda, his older brother John, and six others, all slaves of a man named James Burroughs, a veteran of the War of 1812, who owned a two-hundred-acre farm near a crossroads that featured the tiny post office of Hale's Ford in the foothills of the Blue Ridge Mountains, in an area dotted with similar farms. To call this place a plantation would be to miss the point. It was a small hardscrabble farm far from the myths and realities of a large plantation.

He would later take the name Booker Taliaferro (pro-
nounced Tolliver) Washington, but when he was born on
some rags on the floor of the slave cabin he had only one
name: Booker. As a slave he was worth $400 in 1861, at the
age of five. Of the ten slaves on the Burroughs farm, four
adults and six children, most were in some way related. One
was a strong young farmhand named Lee, the most valuable slave, worth $1,000. Since the entire inventory of farm
equipment, furniture, pots and pans, hoes, rakes, animals,
and slaves on the Burroughs farm was worth about $7,000 in
1860, Lee was a valuable farmhand indeed. Booker's mother,
Jane Ferguson, age forty-one when the Civil War started, was
the farm's cook. She was a sickly woman valued at $250.
She had probably been owned by the Burroughs family since
she was ten. Her half-sister Sophia, about Jane's age, was
also valued at $250. Jane's half-brother, whom Booker called
Uncle Monroe, was a slave on the farm in 1861. He was
about twenty-eight years of age and worth $600.

As a young boy Booker watched as Uncle Monroe was
stripped naked and beaten with a cowhide strap. Reflecting
on his childhood in later years, Washington did not think his
owners were particularly harsh masters. He said the slave
system itself was the burden and the evil, regardless of how
the masters treated their slaves. Being somebody's property
was the awful thing; not being free was the worst part.

Booker's childhood was filled with labor, with little time
for play. By the time he was four or five years old he was
already working as a slave, fetching things and doing chores
that didn't require much strength. One of his regular duties
was to pull the cord for an elaborate overhead fan made of
paper that swept over the Burroughes' dining room table to
keep the flies away. As he grew stronger his workload increased—feeding the farm animals, carrying water from the
well to the men in the fields, sweeping and cleaning. Even

before he had the full strength to do the job, he was sometimes assigned the task of carrying a large bag of corn to a
mill three miles from the farm. If the bag fell from the horse
he was riding, which it did now and then, young Booker did
not have the strength to lift it back onto the horse; he would
have to wait for a passerby to help him. He later said he remembered crying that he was not strong enough to lift the
corn sack. He heard stories that the thick woods he passed
through on the way to the mill were filled with deserters
from the Civil War who would cut off the ears of a black
boy. Worse than that, if he was late bringing the corn back
from the mill, he would surely face a scolding or maybe a
whipping.

Booker's cabin served as the main kitchen for the farm,
so there were always chores to do in preparing meals for the
slaves and the Burroughs family. All cooking was done in
a big open fireplace that kept the cabin hot in summer but
hardly warm enough in winter, given the many holes and
gaps in the cabin door and walls. Washington described the
cabin as having a "cat-hole," a hole built into the wall to let
the cats in and out. He wondered why the cabin was built
with this hole, considering that the cats could crawl in and
out of many other holes in the cabin.

It wasn't until after the Civil War that Booker slept in a
bed. He and his sister and brother slept on a pallet of rags
on the floor. Although the floor was just dirt, some boards
covered the middle of the floor and served as a lid for a deep
hole in the ground, a root cellar for storing sweet potatoes
over the winter months. Sometimes when fetching potatoes
from this cellar, Booker would keep a few and roast them for
himself as a treat.

In 1860 nine members of the Burroughs family lived
on this farm. The start of the Civil War the following year
brought great stress to the farm and its inhabitants. James

Burroughs died in the summer of 1861 at the age sixty-six. Two of his sons enlisted in the Confederate army: one died a prisoner of war in 1865, the other was wounded and returned to the farm in 1864. James Burroughs's widow, Elizabeth, age fifty-nine when the war began, ran the farm until her son Newt returned home in 1864.

The war brought great excitement and apprehension to the slaves on the Burroughs farm, just as it did to the four million slaves on farms, plantations, and cities and towns throughout the South. No aspect of life was left untouched by war, even in areas far away from the battlefields. Talk of freedom was in the air. With the approach of the Union army, thousands of slaves fled from their masters to seek its protection. Most, however, stayed where they were and toughed it out with their masters. Many parts of the South fell into a daily life of survival and subsistence as crops and livestock were confiscated to feed the soldiers of both armies.

Booker would listen to the Burroughs family talk about the Civil War during their meals as he stood silently to the side pulling the cord on the big fan. They complained that they could no longer get things such as coffee, tea, or sugar. Washington would later recall that he thought the slaves didn't suffer as much as the whites because of the war's deprivations, because the slaves were eeking out an existence even before the war. He could not recall a single time when his family had ever sat down and eaten together at a table as the white folks did. Slaves were used to grabbing a morsel here and there, scraping out a cooking pot after the master's family was served, and finding food the way the farm animals did. He grew up living off table scraps. The slaves' main diet was cornbread and fatback pork, which came from the farm and did not depend on outside supplies.

Booker often accompanied the white women of the farm and their neighbors on long horseback rides. He went along to tend their horses when they stopped along the road. Once, he recalled, the ladies stopped to have tea and eat ginger cookies. He had never seen a ginger cookie. He imagined what it might be like to be free and to eat a ginger cookie whenever he wanted one.

Booker's childhood thoughts of what freedom would be like could be expressed as simply as the story of the ginger cookies, or it could be much deeper. He recalled wondering who he was. Even though he was a child, he was developing a sense of what emancipation could mean. Like so many slaves, he dreamed of a different world where he would be free to do things and go places like white people. He saw how hard his mother worked, despite her poor health, and how much effort she expended to care for Booker and his siblings. This motherly attention often manifested itself as a late-night treat—a drumstick or pieces of cake left over from the Burroughes' table—something to ease the hunger. Throughout his whole life Washington would look upon his mother fondly as a saint.

Booker saw his world and the world of the Burroughs family and wondered why they were so different. The Burroughs family all had a variety of clothes to wear, even though the Civil War made new clothes hard to come by. Booker had one piece of clothing—a tow shirt, a pullover top that was long enough to cover his nakedness. It was made of local flax and was itchy and uncomfortable until it was broken in, which sometimes took months. Much of the time until he was six or seven years old Booker simply ran around naked. His first shoes were made of wood, with rough leather tops. These simple but tangible things—a shirt, a pair of shoes—made him feel like he was growing up. Despite the itchiness of the shirt and the discomfort of the shoes, his simple clothes were property that belonged to him.

Booker learned about freedom by listening to the adult slaves who would often gather at night to talk about the war and what it meant to them. They were illiterate, and kept that way by the slave system, but they could nonetheless follow the news of the war with great interest through the "grapevine telegraph"—the spread of news by word of mouth that kept slaves informed about events despite their illiteracy and their isolated rural existence. One day in April 1865, when Booker was nine years old, the slaves learned of General Robert E. Lee's surrender at Appomattox Court House. The war had ended. The word spread quickly among the slaves on neighboring farms. At first they kept quiet about the news and showed no outward display of jubilation. On the Burroughs farm nothing changed for a while— the slaves were uncertain what would happen next.

Not long after the news of Lee's surrender, a man came to the farm, Booker recalled, and all the slaves were told to gather in front of Burroughs's farmhouse. The man, perhaps a local official charged with the task, traveled from farm to farm to read a statement. Booker stood beside his mother with Amanda and John and the other slaves while the man read aloud to them. It was the first public speech Booker had ever heard. He didn't understand much of it at the time, but the message was clear to his mother and the other adult slaves. When the man finished speaking, Jane leaned over, crying, and whispered, "Now, my children, we are free." Slavery was ended. Freedom had arrived.

What happened next on the Burroughs farm was a story repeated with countless variations throughout the South. Some of the adult slaves took to the road to test their freedom. They could now go where they pleased without fear of a "regulator" with a pack of hounds coming to hunt them down and return them to bondage. Some went off and never looked back. Some went in search of family that had been scattered by slavery. Others wandered about for a while, then returned to the same place where they had been slaves.

Although the war ended in April 1865, it was not until August that things began to change for the slaves on the Burroughs farm and for young Booker and his family. Uncle Monroe decided not to leave the area. He took the last name of his master's family, and as Monroe Burroughs hired himself out as a farmhand in Bedford County, Virginia. There is no record of what happened to Lee, the most valuable slave on the farm. He simply disappeared. Booker and his family would soon leave and set out for a new life far from the Burroughs farm.

Booker's mother had a husband, Washington Ferguson, who had been a slave on a nearby farm in Hale's Ford owned by Josiah Ferguson. Jane and "Wash" had been married in 1859 even though there was probably no formal ceremony. Booker was three years old at the time. Wash was the father of Booker's half-sister Amanda. He had been an unruly slave who gave his master fits, so to rid himself of this trouble-maker, Josiah Ferguson rented Wash to others needing slave labor. Wash Ferguson worked on a railroad construction crew and then at the salt furnaces at Kanawha Salines, an industrial area near Charleston, Virginia, before that portion of the state became part of West Virginia in 1863. While Wash Ferguson was working in a tobacco factory in Lynchburg in 1864, Union general David Hunter raided the area before Confederate troops under the command of Jubal Early forced his retreat. During Hunter's retreat Ferguson and many other slaves escaped and followed the Union soldiers to freedom. When the war ended Wash returned to work at the salt furnaces, this time as a free man earning wages in the new state of West Virginia.

Booker had seldom seen his stepfather. Before he ran away from slavery in 1864, Wash rarely visited Jane and the children. Once or twice he had appeared at Christmas, one of the few opportunities in the year when slaves had any time for themselves. But in August 1865 Wash Ferguson sent his family a rented wagon and told them to join him in Malden, West Virginia, the town that had formed near the salt furnaces, along the banks of the Kanawha River, just upstream from Charleston, where they would be united as a family and begin a life together.

Jane packed her meager belongings and her three children on the mule-drawn wagon and said goodbye to slavery and the Burroughs farm. From now on she aimed to cook for her own family and raise her children in freedom. The journey to Malden took ten days of often rough travel and nights camped in the woods along the road. At one point the travelers had to descend from the high cliffs along the New River gorge to the riverbed, cross the river, and push up a steep trail to the heights on the other side. Booker and John walked a good part of the distance while little Amanda rode in the wagon with Jane.

The town of Malden was a new world for young Booker; he had never seen anything like it. He was nervous about what he saw and downright sickened by what he smelled. It was so different from the small farm where he had grown up. The first thing that hit him was the odor of rotting garbage and the smell of human waste. He was used to the smell of a farm and the farm animals, but in this place of crowded cabins with hundreds of persons, the concentration of outhouses left the air with a foul stink. Here blacks and poor whites were thrust together in dwellings that were not much better, if at all, than the slave cabin he had left behind in Virginia. To some extent Malden was divided by race, with many of the black people living in an area called Tinkersville. But Wash Ferguson lived in Malden itself, which had a higher concentration of whites but with blacks mixed in too.

The salt industry, a feature of the area for generations, was limping along by the time the Civil War ended. But it remained a place of employment for newly freed slaves and poor whites alike. Large deposits of salt and underground salt water had once made the Kanawha Salines one of the leading sources of salt for the Cincinnati packing industry in the era before refrigeration, when salt-packing of perishable meat was the only way to preserve it. Deep wells, up to a thousand feet down, brought the salt water to the surface, where it was evaporated and the salt collected and packed into large barrels. Salt packers like Wash Ferguson worked long hours at backbreaking labor and were paid on piece work—the more barrels you filled, the more money you made.

Booker eventually got used to the smell of the place, but he never completely adjusted to the rough-and-tumble aspects of this town of so few refinements. His young eyes, having seen only the small farms along the Blue Ridge Mountains of Virginia, were not yet capable of a sophisticated analysis of his social situation. But he did not like the things he saw in Malden: drinking, fighting, gambling, and what he would latter describe as the regular presence of "shockingly immoral practices" characterized the town. He had never seen so many people crammed into such a small area. They all seemed to live on top of one another in cabins just a few feet apart. He feared white people and thought they were ignorant and degraded. They were no friends of his race.

Washington said little about his stepfather. Washington Ferguson was probably not a cruel man, but the times and circumstances were plenty cruel. Both Booker and John resented the way they felt their stepfather used them. Hardly had Booker and his family settled into their new existence when a new reality hit hard. Early one morning before sunrise, Booker and John were shaken awake by their stepfather and told to get dressed so they could go to work.

Freedom for Booker had been short-lived. He no longer had a master, but he now had a stepfather who made him work for his keep. For all practical purposes, Booker had merely traded one job and one master for another job and another master. And now the work was more difficult than the life he had experienced as a slave. He wondered if this was what freedom was all about—he did not feel free.

Wash Ferguson was simply trying to feed his family. He took his two stepchildren into the salt furnaces with him and showed them how to pack a barrel of salt. It was not just a matter shoveling salt into the barrel; it had to be pounded down until the density of the packed salt reached the required weight to be considered a full barrel. The boys would help Wash pack his barrels. At the end of the long work day an accounting would take place of how many barrels had been filled. Wash Ferguson knew that Booker, nine, and his brother John, eleven, would not pack nearly as much salt as he, but still it would mean more income for the struggling family.

Booker labored long hours with his stepfather and brother in the salt furnaces. He never liked it, in fact he hated it. He resented his stepfather because he saw no future in this never-ending work. He wasn't allowed to keep the wages he earned. How was this different from slavery? Booker had always been inquisitive and a dreamer. He saw things around him that could not be his and wondered why. He yearned to break out of his new world of confinement and labor, and the yearning grew stronger with each passing year. When work at the salt furnaces sometimes slacked, Wash Ferguson would find jobs for Booker and John in the nearby coal mine. The drudgery seemed endless. Booker was a growing boy, made strong and tough by his physical labor, but he could see no future.

The end of slavery made some things possible that had been forbidden. There was, despite his circumstances, a seed of freedom that Booker could nurture. One of the great mysteries that had intrigued him from his earliest memories was the magic of reading, which he knew about from his days in slavery. Laura Burroughs, his particular favorite among his master's family, was a schoolteacher. The white children from the surrounding farms attended school, where they learned to read. Perhaps this was one more thing that whites were allowed to do that he wasn't, and it drove him to want to learn how to read. The day the man came to the Burroughs farm and read aloud that slavery was ended showed him the power of the written word. The first thing Booker learned to read was the number 18 on the salt barrels he filled. This was Wash's assigned number. Booker didn't know any other numbers, but he would write out the number 18 in the dirt with his finger. It was a beginning.

Booker pleaded with his mother to help him learn to read, but Jane was illiterate and could not help him directly. Yet she did something that changed Booker's life: she managed to find a used copy of Noah Webster's spelling book and gave it to her son. It was the best gift he had ever received. The Webster blue-back speller, so called because of the dark blue color of the cover, was used by generations of Americans to learn how to read. By the 1860s it was as common as the Bible and one of the most influential and widely available texts ever published. In addition to its step-by-step lessons, from learning the alphabet to sounding out words by syllables to building vocabulary, the blue-back speller contained moral lessons and fables. It was filled with biblical passages, and it was not lost on the reader that Webster considered the Christian faith to be the bedrock of a successful democratic nation and the key to individual prosperity and salvation.

Booker took to the speller eagerly and began to learn his ABCs and a whole lot more. Through his spelling book he would learn his first lessons in the importance of leading a moral life of Christian virtue. He would learn the magic of storytelling through the fables that accompanied the speller, and he would be introduced to scriptural passages and ideas regarding the value of labor, the importance of an education, the desirability of being liked by others, and the virtues of clean living and humility. In his spelling book Booker found a source of power, a strategy for success, and a road to freedom. He learned lessons in this spelling book that he would never forget, lessons that would later be reinforced by his schooling at Hampton Institute and put into action as he built his very own school.

What Booker learned from that one spelling book would place him in the mainstream of American values that he would share with millions of other Americans who, in one way or another, were exposed to the same little blue-back book. It would become the basis for his entire career as an educator and leader. He spent hours with his book—the only one he owned. He carried it with him wherever he went, even to work, and internalized its message once he got beyond the ABCs and the seemingly never-ending lists of words that he had to learn to pronounce. It was the Bible disguised as a spelling book. He would be influenced by a succession of New Englanders, but the first and foremost of them was none other than Noah Webster, long dead but still reaching new generations though his spelling book first published when George Washington was president of the United States.

One day on the streets of Malden, Booker was deeply moved by the sight of a young black man, one of the workers at the salt furnaces, who was reading aloud from a newspaper to a group of other blacks who could not read for themselves. This man had learned to read in Ohio and had become a regular reader of newspapers for those who couldn't read. Booker could see the power this reader had over people. He watched as the illiterate blacks and whites hung on his every word: he had something the others needed. Booker could see the admiration they had for him. Booker wanted to be like him.

In most places, learning to read had been denied to slaves by law. Keeping slaves illiterate was a method of control in the slave system. Once slavery ended, blacks across the South turned to building their own churches and schools. Both church and school made learning to read a priority, if for no other reason than to be able to read the Bible. But there were other reasons. Booker Washington was not the only newly freed slave who sensed that learning to read and obtaining an education were the best ways to take advantage of freedom. They meant empowerment. The black population of Malden was no different. They wanted a school for black children, and under the leadership of Lewis Rice, a black minister who was himself unable to read and write, the black citizens of Malden set out to find a teacher.

When William Davis, another black man from Ohio who could read, came to town, Reverend Rice convinced him to help form a school in Malden. Davis was twenty years old when he began teaching in Malden. He had received a basic education in Chillicothe, Ohio, and then served two years as a cook in the Union army. At first the Malden school had no real classroom. Davis "boarded around," that is, he visited the homes of the students, whether they were youngsters or adults. The people paid him what they could or fed him a meal. Before long, however, Davis had a place where students could come to him—in Reverend Rice's bedroom, where benches from the church were brought in each day to make a classroom. In 1866, thanks to a West Virginia law that provided state support for free Negro schools, Malden, because of its large black population, eventually acquired an actual schoolroom.

Booker could not wait to attend school, but his stepfather had different plans: Booker could not be spared from his labors at the salt furnaces. He was devastated, but this terrible blow only furthered his desire to read. He studied his blue-back speller with even more determination. Through the intercession of Booker's mother, Wash Ferguson finally relented and allowed Booker to attend night school after he had worked all day packing salt. Booker's mother continued to urge her husband to allow the boy to go to school. The compromise Wash Ferguson made was to allow Booker to attend the day school only after he had arisen at 4 A.M., worked at the salt furnaces for five hours until school opened, and then, after school, returned to salt-packing for two or three more hours in the evening.

The Malden school and its new teacher became Booker's passion. He could tolerate the long hours of work at the salt furnaces because he knew he could also go to school. To attend school Booker needed a first name and a last name. Just how he selected "Washington" to be his last name is unclear, and he himself could never fully explain how he acquired his last and middle names. When the schoolteacher asked what his full name was, he blurted out "Booker Washington." He may have been giving his stepfather's first name, or he may have been thinking of something else entirely, perhaps George Washington. But he clearly did not choose his mother's married name or that of his stepfather, Ferguson. Years later, when asked how he had acquired his middle name, Taliaferro, Washington recalled that his mother said she had given him this name early on. As was the case with so many freed slaves, taking a name—of a former master, a prominent white family in the area, a national leader, another black family, or some other name entirely—was often a complex matter. But a full name of one's choosing was one of the things that came with freedom.

Booker's father was not satisfied with the compromise balancing work and school. He took Booker out of school again and sent him to the coal mine near the salt works. To Booker, the mine was a frightening place. He hated the mile-long journey into its damp and dark. He carried his spelling book with him and tried to study whenever he could by the coal miner's light on his cap. His mother arranged for him to get lessons at night, but the new teacher was no match for William Davis, and Booker quickly tired of him. He didn't seem to know as much as Booker did. Despair flooded in. Booker seemed trapped in the mine with no way out.

Just how long Booker T. Washington worked at the salt furnaces and in the coal mine is not certain. Washington's memory and that of others from that time were not clear, and there is little documentation to support a firm conclusion. The best estimate seems to be that Booker spent about two years, probably to late 1867 or early 1868, at hard labor while he struggled for an education. To a youngster of ten or eleven, this seemed like an eternity.

Jane Ferguson finally found a job for Booker that would get him out of the mine. His stepfather didn't really care where the boy worked as long as he was able to earn a small income for the family. Booker's new job turned out to be a blessing in disguise, but it was a while before the youngster realized this. He was to become a houseboy. Not just any houseboy but an employee of the wealthiest white family with the largest and most elegant house in Malden, General Lewis Ruffner and his wife Viola. Booker thought he knew the difference between life in the slave cabin and life in his master's modest farmhouse. But he had seen nothing to compare with the transition he was about to make. The gulf between the squalid cabins of the salt packers and the coal miners and the fancy home of the Ruffners was far greater than the one he had known earlier. He was about to begin a new kind of journey in which he would see firsthand how a wealthy white family lived. There would be much to learn and see.

Booker left his Malden cabin and moved into the Ruffners' house, where he would come under the strict tutelage of his new employer, Viola Knapp Ruffner, a former New England schoolteacher who was known to Booker by reputation even before he met her. Many other boys around Malden had worked for her, and they told stories of how strict she was and how difficult it was to please her. It seems she was moody and complained a lot. Booker looked on his new job with considerable apprehension.

The new houseboy received his board and six dollars a month for his work. The cash went directly to his stepfather. His duties as a houseboy consisted of a wide variety of chores: cleaning, sweeping, running errands, and, when crops were in season, taking grapes, peaches, and other farm produce to the cabins in Malden and Tinkersville and selling them door to door. Mrs. Ruffner was a stickler for punctuality, neatness, and good work habits. Her brusque New England accent added to her stern and sour demeanor.

At one point early on in his work as a domestic servant, Booker decided he had had enough: he ran away. He convinced a steamboat captain to hire him to wait tables on the run from Malden to Cincinnati, and off he went. When the captain found that Booker had no experience waiting tables, he planned to put him off the boat long before it reached Cincinnati. But Booker persuaded the captain to let him ride to Cincinnati and then back to Malden. He returned to Mrs. Ruffner, apologized, asked for his job back, and got it.

Booker and Mrs. Ruffner grew to be friends even though there were many times that he felt frustrated with her. Still, he came to understand and admire her. He worked for her intermittently for about four years, performing well and learning how to please her. He came to see that her strictness, her concern for punctuality, and her desire for absolute cleanliness were important parts of her upbringing. She was not making demands just to torture him; it was what she expected of herself and anyone who worked for her. She had come from a poor family with seven children. She had taught school in New England for meager wages until she read an advertisement that General Ruffner was looking for a governess. She applied for the job and got it, and before long General Ruffner proposed marriage.

Washington learned much from this former schoolteacher from New England. He would later say that Mrs. Ruffner played an important role in his general education. She allowed him to attend school part of the day so that he could continue his schooling. She embodied the Puritan work ethic of her New England ancestors, and Washington learned much from her personal habits of honesty, thrift, hard work, punctuality, cleanliness, and good manners. He also learned new words from her and a manner of speaking that he would later develop into strong oratorical skills. Young Booker did not know it at the time, but the Ruffners would be the first of a series of rich white people who would play key roles in his later rise to prominence as an educator and race leader.

CHAPTER TWO

The Power of Education

*Perhaps the most valuable thing that I got out of my second
year [at Hampton] was an understanding of the use and value
of the Bible.*—Booker T. Washington, *Up from Slavery, 1901*

🙟 Booker Washington matured quickly. He had worked
literally all of his young life. His ability to read and write
gave him an advantage, a magical skill, not possessed by
most of the others who worked the salt furnaces and coal
mines around Malden, West Virginia. His education would
be his road to salvation and true emancipation.

During his seven years in Malden, Washington grew to
be a strong young man. What set him apart from many of the
other young black men in Malden was his sense of purpose
and his dogged pursuit to better himself. He recalled ponder-
ing his future if he were to stay in Malden. Would he end up
like his stepfather, working endlessly at manual labor with
little chance ever to advance? Could this young man ever
break the cycle of life that had been set in slavery and per-
petuated in poverty?

Washington's intermittent education at the Tinkersville
Colored School, his nocturnal tutors, his first black teacher,
William Davis, the Sabbath school of Reverend Lewis Rice,
and his employment as a domestic servant for a former New
England schoolteacher had helped him along the way, but no

single experience, or even these taken together, was enough to break the chains that bound him to a life of manual labor.

Poverty is always a formidable barrier to overcome. Hard work alone was not enough for Booker to achieve his goals. There were simply too few opportunities for a black man or woman other than manual labor: the doors to most occupations were closed to blacks. Two other socially acceptable avenues of employment for a black man besides manual labor were preaching and teaching. Washington saw glimmers of yet another profession that might be open to him when in 1872 he became secretary of a local black Republican club in Tinkersville.

Washington's coming of age occurred during Reconstruction, that period of American history following the Civil War that was marked by massive social and economic revolution and a major adjustment in politics and race relations. It is difficult to know what he realized of the revolutionary forces that were sweeping the nation. Just as a solider in battle knows only the war as it appears in front of his own nose, Booker saw but a small part of what was happening in Reconstruction America. Yet from his limited perspective in rural West Virginia, what he saw was typical of life throughout the South. Booker's town of Malden was not immune to the kind of racial violence sweeping the rest of the South during Reconstruction.

Before and during the Civil War, blacks who worked the Kanawha Salines were mostly slaves. But once the war was over the white population had to face the fact that black workers required wages for their efforts. It was a large adjustment for both sides. Violence was no stranger in hardscrabble places like Malden, and interracial violence was particularly ugly. Brawls between whites and blacks—the kind that often occurred after the consumption of too much

liquor—took on new urgency as whites attempted to dominate blacks as they had during slavery days. But things were
different now. Many whites concluded that the only way to
keep blacks "in their place" was through intimidation, repression, and violence.

During Booker's first full year of freedom, a homegrown
American terrorist group, the Ku Klux Klan, organized itself in Pulaski, Tennessee, and elected former Confederate
general Nathan Bedford Forrest, a onetime plantation owner
and slave trader as its first grand wizard. The Klan was composed largely of former Confederate soldiers and officers. In
different places in the South it was known by various names
in a loose association of similar organizations. The Klan and
its many imitators ushered in an era of mayhem, murder,
and intimidation designed to drive black voters from the
polls and to ensure white supremacy in the South. These
terrorists often hid their identities under hoods and robes
and ran rampant through parts of the South during Washington's formative years, until in the early 1870s the federal
government put an end to most of the Klan violence.

Even after the Klan ceased to be a direct threat to most
blacks in the South, its legacy of intimidation remained. With
the Klan all but disbanded and blatant vigilantism by armed
night riders quelled, the job of keeping blacks "in their place"
fell to those who did not wear the hooded robes of the Klans-
men. Racial intimidation, segregation, and the denial of civil
rights were fostered by elected officials at all levels, from the
local sheriff to legislators and state governors, who openly
espoused white supremacy. The white opinion makers of the
South, the editors of Southern newspapers, kept up a daily
barrage of editorials that attacked any blacks who were active in politics. They argued with no subtlety or decorum
that "nigger rule" was the most horrible thing to come out of
the Civil War, and that it was the duty of white Southerners

to save civilization through white supremacy. For his entire life Booker Washington lived in an America dominated by the idea of white supremacy in all things political, social, and economic. He would have to find a way to grow his ambition within the stark realities of pervasive racism.

One payday Saturday Booker was eyewitness to an incident that escalated into a riot and dramatically bought home to him just how explosive was racial tension in his corner of the world. He would never forget this incident. It helped shape his entire philosophy on how to deal with a world so hostile to his race. It was Saturday, December 4, 1869, when a fight broke out between a white man and a black man on a Malden street. The black man won; the white man swore he'd get even and threatened the black man's life. The black man, Tom Preston, thereupon had a warrant issued against his assailant. This simple act on the part of Tom Preston—seeking the law to resolve the matter—struck at the heart of white supremacists who feared the power that former slaves might gain through legal means. John Fewell, the white man in the fight, had friends who were members of a local Klan who called themselves Gideon's Band. They swore that no black man would take a white man before a justice of the peace.

The next day, as Tom Preston walked the road from Tinkersville to Malden to file his complaint, he was surrounded by ten friends armed with pistols to make sure he arrived in town in one piece. They were met by a group of armed whites accompanied by John Fewell, who ordered the black men to return to Tinkersville. After one of the whites threw a brick that hit a black man, shots were fired. The black men retreated a short distance to some cover.

Meanwhile, hearing the gunshots from his home, General Lewis Ruffner, accompanied by his houseboy, thirteen-year-old Booker Washington, ran the short distance down the lane to the place of the fight. Booker stood on the side-lines and watched as General Ruffner, the owner of the salt furnaces where these men worked, tried to stop the fight. His presence caused the men to pause. The blacks put down their arms and followed behind the general as he confronted the white men. When one of the whites threw a brick that hit Ruffner in the head and knocked him unconscious, the fight resumed.

Both sides fired at each other until they ran out of am-munition, then resorted to rocks and bricks. Two white men were wounded. General Ruffner, who was carried from the fight to his home, turned out to be the most seriously in-jured in the struggle. None of the ten black men were badly hurt in the fight, and none was wounded by gunfire.

Later that night a small army of about two hundred Klansman rode their horses into Tinkersville looking for the men who had participated in the gunfight. Luckily for the blacks in Tinkersville, those who fought that day hid themselves. A grand jury eventually investigated the inci-dent, but its findings were inconclusive. Most of the Klans-men refused to testify because they claimed they could not violate their oath of secrecy. The grand jury did conclude, however, that the Klan's purpose in this incident was to de-prive the black man of his right to use the courts—or, as one witness testified, "to clean out and finish up the niggers at Tinkersville."

Washington would later write how discouraged he was by this incident. How could he, or any other member of his race, follow the law if white men could threaten them every time they tried to use the law to address their grievances? Law and politics seemed to be the exclusive province of whites. The only chance for success for a young black man trying to find his way in the world, Booker thought, was to get an education and use it to find a job that would provide a way out of poverty. To achieve this much would be a triumph. It would mean that blacks could earn the respect of their white oppressors, a respect that might lead to the end of oppression and the beginning of acceptance in the daily affairs of both races.

While searching for a way to gain more schooling and get out of Malden, Booker had overheard a conversation in the coal mine. Two black miners had been talking about a new school for Negroes—Hampton Institute in Virginia—where blacks could get room and board and an education by working at the school. It sounded almost too good to be true. In 1871 Booker's first teacher, William Davis, moved to Charleston and was replaced at the Tinkersville school by a graduate of Hampton, Henry Clay Payne. This new teacher furthered Booker's interest in Hampton. Before long everyone in Malden and Tinkersville knew that Booker Washington wanted to go to Hampton—it was just about all he talked about. He knew little about the school, which had been established just a few years earlier in 1868 and was run by a retired Union general, Samuel Chapman Armstrong.

In the fall of 1872, Booker Washington set out on the biggest journey of his life. He was going to Hampton, five hundred miles from Malden. The trek was to be an adventure in itself. Booker had very little money to make the journey, and he worried about leaving Malden with his mother in poor health. But destiny called, it was time to go. His half-brother John encouraged him, and so did his mother. His stepfather seemed resigned to the fact that Booker had to leave. The church Booker attended, Reverend Rice's Baptist church, helped a little. Members of the congregation, proud of their young church secretary, passed the hat and gave him a few nickels and dimes to help him on his way.

At sixteen years of age Booker left Malden in style, with clean clothes and a carpetbag with a few belongings. He boarded the train at Charleston, waved goodbye, and started the first and easiest leg of his journey. The Chesapeake and Ohio tracks ran only part of the way, so Booker left the train halfway through the journey and switched to stagecoaches. He was the only black passenger on one leg of the stage-coach trip when it reached a hotel for the night. Because the hotel would not give him a room or feed him, he remained huddled outside in the cold fall air until he could board the stagecoach again the next morning.

Eventually he reached Richmond, Virginia, capital of the old Confederacy, just eighty miles short of his destination. It was late at night when the stage pulled in. Booker was cold, dirty, out of money, and had no place to stay. Richmond was the biggest city he had ever seen, and without money in his pocket it seemed to him cold and hostile. He tried to find a place to sleep but was turned away several times. He passed stores with pies and fried chicken, but they were beyond his reach. He spent the night hungry, under a boardwalk, sleep-ing with his carpetbag as a pillow.

The next morning he wandered along the docks until he found some men unloading pig iron and convinced the ship's captain to let him work to earn breakfast. Washington had a winning way about him. He was eager and forthright and good at selling himself to others. The white captain took a liking to Booker and put him to work. Booker spent several days, perhaps a week or more, working as a stevedore on the Richmond docks and continued sleeping under the board-walk until he had saved enough money to complete the last leg of his journey. He later recalled that he had exactly fifty cents when he reached Hampton Normal and Agricultural Institute.

Hampton Institute was not much to look at in 1872, but to young Booker, whose only experience with a school build-ing was the modest one-room school in Malden, the three-

Academic Hall at Hampton Normal and Agricultural Institute as it appeared in 1872. *(Hampton University)*

story brick building called Academic Hall seemed like a castle that rose up along the flat Virginia tidewater with a view of Hampton Roads harbor. He later wrote in his autobiography, *Up from Slavery*, that "It seemed to me to be the largest and most beautiful building I had ever seen. The sight of it seemed to give me new life." The school sat on land that was once a plantation called Little Scotland. During the Civil War it had become a safe gathering place for blacks. Rudimentary classes, taught by a black woman, Mary Smith Peake, were held there for a while beginning in 1861. In 1863 the Emancipation Proclamation was read there under the branches of a sturdy oak tree. Here was where General Armstrong organized his new school in 1868. It was officially chartered in 1870, just two years before Booker arrived.

The first person Booker encountered at Hampton was a white teacher, Mary Mackie, the lady principal of the school, a Yankee from Newburgh, New York, who had come south to teach the newly freed slaves. Booker must have been quite a sight. He had not had a bath or a haircut in a month. His clothes were dirty, and he was tired from his long journey. Miss Mackie gave him a room in one of the military barracks that the school had taken over, which had been part of Camp Hamilton during the war, not far from Fort Monroe. He cleaned himself up and returned to her office.

Booker Washington's entrance exam for his admission to Hampton Institute made for a story he told again and again throughout his life. It appeared in both his autobiographies written many years later. It became a part of his legend that emphasized his humble origins and suggested how far he progressed during his lifetime. Miss Mackie, still not sure if he was fit for admission to the school, gave Booker a broom and told him to go into an adjoining room and sweep it. His thoughts flashed back to his time as the houseboy of another Yankee schoolmarm, Viola Ruffner. If there was one task he had mastered in his youth, it was sweeping and cleaning. He had learned how to please and to impress a stickler for cleanliness like Mrs. Ruffner. He was confident he could do it again. He cleaned and dusted the room so well that Miss Mackie, after a thorough, militarylike inspection, could not find a speck of dust. She admitted him to the school and gave him a job as janitor of Academic Hall to help pay his tuition and expenses. "I was one of the happiest souls on earth," Washington later wrote. "The sweeping of that room," he wrote, "was my college examination, and never did any youth pass an examination for entrance into Harvard or Yale that gave him more genuine satisfaction."

Washington soon settled into his routine at school. He would rise at four o'clock in the morning to get the firewood and light the fireplaces in Academic Hall, attend his classes, and then work into the night cleaning the same building. He slept in a barracks room with six other students where for the first time he learned how to sleep between two sheets on a bed. He had never had a bed with regular sheets, and he did not know that one slept between the sheets rather than underneath both until he saw how other students did it. The food at the school was meager but adequate. Washington remembered that his diet consisted mostly of corn-bread and perhaps once a week some white bread. Students drank coffee and tea from yellow bowls. The dining tables had no tablecloths.

Hampton Normal and Agricultural Institute was not a college in the way we think of such institutions today, or in the way Hampton itself evolved into the present-day Hampton University. In Booker Washington's time Hampton was one of a number of schools established to train black teachers in the skills necessary to be successful in a predominantly agricultural world. It was a secondary school, not a college at all, and quite a rudimentary institution. But it was growing rapidly, and what it lacked in facilities it made up for in the zeal of its teachers. The school library was virtually nonexistent when Washington arrived and depended on donations of used books from Northern supporters. The school had fewer than twenty faculty and staff, but it had grown from an initial enrollment of twenty students in 1868 to well over one hundred by the time Washington arrived. When Washington graduated three years later, almost two hundred students boarded at the school.

Hampton had two basic missions: to help prepare students to become teachers, and to prepare them for a life of agricultural pursuits and the business skills necessary for success. Academic courses stressed basic subjects like spelling, reading, English grammar, and rhetoric and composition. Students learned arithmetic and basic algebra. They studied U.S. History, English history, and English writers.

The curriculum included geography courses, botany, the science of civil government, bookkeeping, and plenty of Bible lessons.

The agricultural program included crop rotation, soils, market gardening, more bookkeeping, and a course on how to prepare business letters and legal documents. Students could also learn printing in the school's print shop, and female students took courses in the Girls' Industrial Department, where they learned to use a variety of sewing machines and mastered other "household industries." It cost ten dollars a month to attend Hampton in those days. If you were able-bodied you were expected to pay half in cash and work for the other half. Students usually earned from five to ten cents an hour working at the school; labor was an essential part of the school's ethic. The school catalog described work as required for "purposes of discipline and instruction." Allowances were made for students who had other jobs, especially those whose salaries were needed to help with family income. Some of these were part-time students who had full-time jobs elsewhere.

The school's principal, General Armstrong, also insisted on strict military discipline. Students participated in drills and guard duty, they marched in columns to and from class, and their clothes were regularly inspected. No "ardent spirits" or tobacco were tolerated. Letters written home were inspected by faculty before they could be mailed. Students could be expelled if they were deficient in their studies, their school jobs, or their personal conduct. Daily devotional services were mandatory, and on Sunday students were required to attend morning services at the public chapel in the nearby National Cemetery, Sunday school in the afternoon, and an evening lecture.

Hampton had been founded as an American Missionary Association (AMA) school. Founded in 1846 by anti-slavery groups and run by the Congregational church, its mission was the education and religious instruction of slaves and then, following emancipation, of freedmen. The AMA also launched schools for Indians and had outposts in Africa. Although often harassed by Southern white opposition to the creation of black schools, AMA teachers played a vital role in bringing education to blacks in the South.

Hampton's board of trustees included only one Southerner, Robert W. Hughes, a former editor of the *Richmond Examiner* and a staunch secessionist who had supported the Confederacy. After the war he had a change of heart and became a moderate Republican and a supporter and friend of President Ulysses Grant. In the South Hughes was branded a Judas, "worse than a carpetbagger" for his switch of loyalties. The president of the Hampton board of trustees, George Whipple of New York City, was an ordained Congregational minister who had been a fervent abolitionist for decades before the Civil War. The board included General Otis Oliver Howard, founder of Howard University, head of the Freedmen's Bureau, and the man in charge of the federal government's efforts to aid blacks in the South. Hampton's treasurer, also a board member, was James F. B. Marshall of Boston, quartermaster general of Massachusetts' state militia. Another trustee, James A. Garfield of Hiram, Ohio, was a Union major general, congressman, and later, in 1881, President of the United States.

Hampton's founding represented both the spirit and reality of the Christian zeal that was a hallmark of the abolitionist movement. Hampton also advanced the agenda of the Republican party and Union victors who now had the task of addressing the overwhelming needs of four million recently freed slaves, among them a young man named Booker T. Washington. There is little evidence that Washington had even a clue of all that Hampton Institute represented and all the forces and players in Reconstruction that were assembled there when he first dreamed of attending the school. But he had in fact arrived at a pivotal place at a pivotal time in the life of the nation. He slept in a Civil War barracks and attended a school run by former Civil War generals, Congregational ministers, abolitionists, and leaders of the Republican party. His teachers were white Northern men and women, not much different from the first white teacher he ever encountered, Viola Ruffner of Malden, West Virginia, by way of Arlington, Vermont.

All these circumstances and people would have their influence on Washington, but none would equal the powerful impact of one man, the school's principal, the dashing, handsome, thirty-three-year-old General Samuel Chapman Armstrong. In many ways Armstrong became the father that Booker Washington never had. The biographer Louis Harlan entitled his chapter on Washington's Hampton experience "Great White Father," to suggest the mesmerizing hold Armstrong had on the young man. Harlan wrote, "General Armstrong was a charismatic figure, whose every gesture was marked down for emulation." Washington quickly began to shape his personal life and habits after those of his hero, a man who had ridden into his life on a white horse and entered his very soul. Washington would later pattern his own school, Tuskegee Institute, after Hampton, and would ride around the campus on horseback inspecting his domain, much as he had watched General Armstrong do at Hampton.

Washington met the general in the first few days after he arrived at Hampton. Armstrong was the youngest of the Civil War generals, a tall, lean, blond-haired man with a rigid military bearing and an aura of moral superiority that he cultivated and maintained his entire life. He had been born in Hawaii in 1839, the son of Christian missionaries in

Samuel Chapman Armstrong, principal of Hampton, exerted a powerful influence on Washington.

the Hawaiian Islands. His firsthand observation of the Hilo Manual Labor School for Hawaiian boys shaped his conception of a similar school for the freedmen.

Armstrong attended Williams College where he was tutored by one of the leading educators and philosophers of education, Mark Hopkins. He volunteered for the Union army in 1862, and at Harpers Ferry his regiment was captured and paroled in the West. He and his men were exchanged in time to take part in the battle of Gettysburg. He ended the war with the rank of colonel, in command of Negro troops. He was breveted as a brigadier general and after the war he worked under General O. O. Howard as a Freedmen's Bureau agent and superintendent of a string of black schools in ten counties in eastern Virginia before applying to the American

Missionary Association to establish a school at Hampton. Armstrong turned down several offers from General Howard to become president of Howard University in Washington, D.C., and spent the rest of his life as principal of Hampton Institute, where he died in 1893.

When Booker Washington first laid eyes on General Armstrong, "he made an impression upon me of being the most perfect specimen of man, physically, mentally and spiritually, that I had ever seen. . . ." Washington wrote that he had complete confidence in General Armstrong; he could not imagine the general failing at anything he decided to do. Years later he reflected that the best part of his education at Hampton "was obtained by being permitted to look upon General Armstrong day by day." Armstrong had the same effect on many Hampton students and teachers, all of whom had the greatest admiration and respect for him.

Washington was not long into his tenure at Hampton before the janitor of Academic Hall became a leader among the students. He was particularly good at debating and seldom missed an opportunity to participate in several of Hampton's debating societies. Virtually every waking hour at the school was accounted for in General Armstrong's spartan regimen. But Washington found twenty minutes just after supper and evening prayers, before mandatory evening study, and organized a society that would gather to discuss important topics and world events.

One of his favorite teachers, Miss Nathalie Lord of Portland, Maine, who was twenty-six years old when she arrived at Hampton in 1873, taught Sunday school and the Bible. She trained Washington in the skills he could derive from knowing the Good Book. It was essential not only for its spiritual value, Washington said, but as literature. He would later have a brief fling as a seminary student and would teach Sunday school and preach sermons throughout his life

Washington as a student at Hampton Institute, ca. 1873. *(Library of Congress)*

even though he was never ordained. He saw how quoting the Bible had a powerful impact in public speaking and debating. Thus this pragmatic man eagerly studied the Bible because he found it so useful. Miss Lord coached Washington in public speaking, tutored him privately, worked on his breathing control, his timing, his inflections, until he excelled at it. In a time when public oratory was still a high art form, Washington understood its power and appreciated how Miss Lord was helping him.

When Washington graduated from Hampton in 1875 his certificate of achievement said he was now qualified to teach a "graded school." He had grown immensely in his three years at Hampton. A good public speaker and debater, he was now a disciplined, self-assured man. At commencement he was featured as one of two students who debated the wisdom of annexing Cuba to the United States. He impressed the distinguished Northern guests and journalists assembled that day with his vigorous opposition to annexing Cuba. A reporter for the *Springfield Republican*, a Massachusetts paper, wrote: "Booker Washington, a mulatto, made a very terse, logical, lawyer-like argument. . . ."

The newly minted graduate still did not know what he planned to do with his certificate from Hampton, but his future seemed brighter than it had when he left Malden three years earlier. Still, he did not have a job, and the nation's economic situation was gloomy. The Panic of 1873, a serious depression, was still reverberating through the land. In his hometown of Malden, things were only growing worse as the salt industry continued its long decline.

Washington needed to earn some money before going home again to a teaching job that awaited him in Tinkersville in the fall. He went north and found work as a waiter, probably at the brand-new United States Hotel in Saratoga Springs, New York, one of the largest hotels in the country. Hampton Institute sent a number of its graduates to this and other hotels in the North where waiters were always needed. Apparently Washington, despite three years at Hampton, with all his newfound confidence, was a flop as a waiter. Customers complained of his ineptness, and he was reduced to being a busboy for a while until he could master the waiter's responsibilities.

After returning home to Malden in the fall of 1875, Washington went to Charleston to be examined for his state teaching credentials. He qualified to teach with a first-grade certificate, which paid less than a higher grade. Although

West Virginia was among the first to set up schools for blacks after the Civil War, black teachers received lower pay than white teachers, and the school year for black schools was a month shorter than that for white schools. Washington's salary was meager—about $31 a month, 25 percent less than a comparable white male teacher would make.

Throwing himself into his work, Washington spent long hours each day on the job, eventually starting a night school. He was not simply teaching the three Rs. He brought with him the Hampton philosophy of personal uplift through better hygiene—bathing, brushing teeth, keeping hair neat, and wearing clean clothes. Throughout his career as an educator, Washington would argue that personal grooming and cleanliness were just as important as book learning. He learned the gospel of the toothbrush at Hampton, carried it back to Malden, and never stopped talking about its importance throughout his years as principal of Tuskegee Institute. Nothing was a better civilizing agent, he said on numerous occasions, than the toothbrush.

Just when Washington's mind fully awakened to the idea that his advancement was tied to that of his race is hard to determine. It can be argued that it happened during his teaching experience in Malden, where his methods were designed for the entire community as much as they were for his students. Hampton had instilled in him a sense of a larger mission. He did not just teach; he started a library, organized a reading room, taught Sunday school, helped students get into Hampton, created a debating society, became active in local politics, and wrote articles and letters to the editors of newspapers, all with the goal of racial uplift.

One of his earliest forays into public speaking on a political issue occurred in 1877, on the question of the location of West Virginia's capital. The state legislature put to the voters the matter of placing a permanent capital in Wheeling or in Charleston. Not surprisingly, Washington favored nearby Charleston. Local white politicians, eager to have a large black turnout for the vote, asked Washington to speak to black audiences in the area. During the summer months that year he spoke at rallies in towns around Charleston. His was a safe position to take, since both whites and blacks around Charleston would benefit from having the capital in their area. In some cases Washington spoke to a racially mixed audience. Newspaper accounts praised his style and his delivery, noting that he included interesting anecdotes to reinforce his argument. He was labeled a "champion of Charleston."

That same summer Washington wrote a lengthy letter to the editor of the *Charleston West Virginia Journal* on the question of how to improve his race. He began with a humbling reference to himself that would make him acceptable to white readers. "This question has presented itself to me, 'can we not improve?' I mean the colored people, for I am a colored man myself, or rather a boy." He was twenty-one when he wrote the editorial—hardly a boy, but he certainly understood that to whites all black men remained boys. His theme was that blacks needed to improve their education. Parents of black children had to be aware of the importance of schooling. "Our many friends," he wrote, "who have stood by us, want to see us accomplish something of ourselves." Poverty was no excuse for not seeking an education. Washington cited the example of Abraham Lincoln, who had grown up in a humble log cabin and had become president of the United States. He was critical of his own people, too, many of whom "spend too great a portion of their time in street walking or in vain or vile talk." He concluded with the idea that "If the colored man will only improve his opportunities and persevere, I believe the time is not far distant when a great portion of them will be equal in education, equal in wealth, equal in civilization, and equal in everything that tends toward human advancement, to any nation or people on earth."

This message, expressed in a hundred different ways over more than three decades, would be Washington's message to the world. His understanding of the solution to race progress and racial harmony with whites had been formed early in his life, and he would not change his message for the remainder of his career. What did change was his skill in delivering this advice and the enlarged platform he would achieve as a prominent educator and race leader.

CHAPTER THREE

The Tuskegee Idea

Before going to Tuskegee I had expected to find there a building and all the necessary apparatus ready for me to begin teaching. To my disappointment I found nothing of the kind. I did find, though, that which no costly building and apparatus can supply—hundreds of hungry, earnest souls who wanted to secure knowledge.—Booker T. Washington, *Up from Slavery,* 1901

Washington survived four challenging years of teaching in Malden, West Virginia. He later wrote that this was one of the happiest times of his life, putting the most favorable spin on his efforts there. But it was also a time of frustration for a man of his ambition and restlessness. He often said that poverty was no excuse for failing in life, but he realized that poverty made success that much harder, and Malden was indeed a poor, isolated place. It was time to move on again. The question was, in which direction? He was still not sure what he wanted to do with his life. His speaking engagements had sparked in him an interest in law, but he did not see how he could carry out the Hampton mission as a lawyer, and that thought persistently nagged him.

He left Malden in 1878 to enter Wayland Seminary, a small Baptist theological school in Washington, D.C., where he explored the possibility of becoming a preacher. He spent the good part of a year there taking courses in theology. Not much is known about his experience at Wayland because Washington seldom referred to it, and the school's records were lost in a fire. His personal views on religion are hard to fathom. He rarely wrote or spoke privately about it. His voluminous private correspondence shows no interest in religion. References to God were rare and fell into the category of generalized platitudes, not much beyond "God bless you." His religious values were expressed publicly, not privately. He often quoted the Bible in speeches, and in countless public forums his broad-gauged nondenominational Christianity was on display. He read the Bible, attended church regularly most of his life, and taught Sunday school. Eventually he would speak in churches in many parts of the country and would give regular talks on Sunday evenings at the nondenominational chapel he established at Tuskegee Institute.

His biographer Louis Harlan speculates that Wayland Seminary may have been too intellectual and urbane for Washington's rural temperament. His practical approach to Christianity was rooted in Webster's blue-back speller and reinforced in Bible classes at Hampton. Christianity was about being a good person, seeking virtue, and wanting to help others. His faith was biblical and missionary inspired, it was not founded on advanced theology. Theologians, after all, were intellectuals and academics, and Washington doubted the practical value of theology. He saw that Christianity had a practical, strategic benefit for him and his people. Talking theology would not put food on the table nor help poor blacks earn a dollar. But living a virtuous life, working hard, being honest, and practicing the Golden Rule would help a farmer or a businessman lead a better life. Christianity had another stark utility for Washington: it was the white man's religion. Espousing Christian values was important for social acceptance. Later he would use his Christianity to loosen the purse strings of Northern congregations in support of black education.

Speaking before a Unitarian conference in Saratoga, New York, in 1886, Washington declared, "My people at the South want to be taught every day practical religion rather than religious dogmas and abstruse doctrine—that it is better to be a Christian man a Methodist or a Baptist to save a soul than subscribe to a creed." He could, at times, be highly critical of black preachers who he thought were more like snake-oil salesmen than men of God. He expressed disdain for so-called doctors among black ministers, with their flamboyant style and sense of self-importance. In 1890 he issued a blistering attack on black preachers in the South, saying, ". . . I have no hesitancy in asserting that three-fourths of the Baptist ministers and two-thirds of the Methodists are unfit, either mentally or morally, or both, to preach the Gospel to any one or to attempt to lead any one."

In 1879 General Samuel Chapman Armstrong invited Washington back to Hampton to give a postgraduate address at the May commencement. Washington eagerly accepted and traveled to Hampton three weeks in advance of his speech to write it and practice it under the tutelage of his former speech teacher, Nathalie Lord. He looked forward to this opportunity because he felt he was a changed man and that everyone would notice. He was no longer the ragged, unpolished teenager who had appeared on Hampton's doorstep just five years earlier. He later wrote in *Up from Slavery* about his triumphal return to Hampton, "I think I may say, without seeming egotism, that it is seldom that five years have wrought such a change in the life and aspirations of an individual."

He called his speech "The Force That Wins," and he delivered it to a rapt audience. Washington's conviction and charisma carried the day, even though the speech was filled with platitudes. Drawing on his teaching experience, he advised, "There is a force with which we can labor and succeed and there is a force with which we can labor and fail." The force that wins came from common sense, right thinking, and trust in God. The goal was not in planning but in doing—not talking about noble deeds but doing them. Newspaper accounts of the speech praised Washington as an exemplar of Hampton's program. It was the most important talk in his budding career as an educator.

Two weeks later General Armstrong offered Washington a teaching job at Hampton. The school was beginning to hire black teachers and Washington saw this as an opportunity, even though the salary was poor. It would give him a chance to further his studies and at the same time be with his sweetheart, Fanny Norton Smith, whom he had known since they were both children in Malden. Two years younger than Washington, Fanny had been born in Malden, West Virginia, in 1858. Her father was part Shawnee, and the few existing photographs of Fanny show her to be a light-skinned woman with pleasant features, an oval face, and high cheekbones, perhaps hinting at her Indian heritage. When Washington returned to Malden to teach school in 1875, she became one of his students. He encouraged her to go to Hampton, and with his help she was admitted there but fell behind in her tuition payments and had to drop out. She returned to Malden in 1878, where she began teaching school with the goal of paying off her debts and returning to Hampton. From her meager salary as a teacher it took her almost two years to save the $48 she needed to clear her account. Once she did, the school's treasurer, J. F. B. Marshall, placed her on the honor roll of those who had paid their school debts from money earned as a teacher. The paths of Washington and Fanny Smith crossed again at Hampton in 1880 and 1881, where they courted and planned to marry as soon as she graduated.

Washington settled in as a night school teacher, attempting to teach basic skills such as reading and writing to eager

Fanny Norton Smith, whom Washington had known from childhood, became his first wife in 1882. *(Tuskegee University)*

men and women who came to classes after working eleven hours. They attended night school from 7 to 9:30 P.M. out of a strong desire to learn. Washington was inspired by their efforts. Under his direction enrollment increased and night school became a feature of Hampton. Most night students managed to advance to the day classes and succeed there. One of the school officials labeled Washington's students the "Plucky Class." The term stuck and became a source of pride.

The 1880s was a time of educational experimentation in the United States, and Hampton Institute found itself in the midst of a new program to acculturate Native Americans. Washington received a new job as supervisor of the "Wigwam," a dormitory for Indian boys. The first Indians to arrive were prisoners of war from the ongoing "pacification" of the Western frontier. The idea had long been brewing among missionary leaders and their military counterparts that the "savage" Indians needed to be civilized. The irony of sending Indians to a black school to learn the white man's ways was lost on General Armstrong and his best pupil, Booker Washington. To them it seemed a natural extension of the Hampton philosophy of racial uplift through education, discipline, and Christianity. If Hampton could help lift blacks out of bondage through Christian zeal and a basic education, there was no reason to believe it would not also work for Indians. Captain Richard Pratt, who would later found the school for Indians at Carlisle, Pennsylvania, on the Hampton model, accompanied the first group of Indian prisoners to Hampton Institute.

To educators like Armstrong, whose parents had been missionaries in Hawaii, the acculturation of Native Americans was merely a matter of teaching another group of people how to be Christian and white. It was the best way to bring them into the fold of useful citizenship. Indians trained at Hampton would return to their reservations and spread the Hampton gospel. Armstrong's choice of Washington as their dormitory supervisor, Louis Harlan suggested, would allow the Indians to "learn better the white man's values and style of life from a black man who had internalized them." Armstrong saw Washington as a superb example of what Hampton could do for black Americans. He had taken a young man born in slavery and shaped him into a person who embodied Armstrong's missionary vision to bring civilization to "backward" races, with altruism and concern for the less fortunate. Washington also internalized Armstrong's belief that blacks were uncivilized, or less civilized, and needed to be trained to be like whites before the race could assume its full place in the affairs of the nation and the world.

In a later account of his work with Indians in *Up from Slavery*, Washington makes no mention that the first Indians to arrive at Hampton were prisoners of battles on the Western frontier. He reports merely that General Armstrong secured from reservations "over one hundred wild and for the most part perfectly ignorant Indians." As their "house-father," Washington was determined to succeed even though he thought the Indians considered themselves superior to him because he was black and had once been a slave. Once Washington got to know his charges, he came to see them pretty much "like any other human beings." What they most disliked about Hampton "were to have their long hair cut, to give up the wearing of their blankets, and to cease smoking." Tellingly, Washington added, "no white American ever thinks that any other race is wholly civilized until he wears the white man's clothes, eats the white man's food, speaks the white man's language, and professes the white man's religion."

On one occasion Washington had to accompany a sick Indian student to the Department of the Interior in Washington so that he could be returned to his reservation. In what he called the "curious workings of caste in America," he and the Indian waited on a steamboat while white passengers ate before he took the Indian to the dining room. There he was told that the Indian could be served but not him. Washington was vexed by this drawing of the color line. When they arrived at their hotel in the nation's capital, again the Indian was lodged but Washington was turned away.

Washington believed that he had great success with the Indian students and that they adapted well to the education they received at Hampton. He wrote a series of articles, "Incidents of Indian Life at Hampton," for the school newspaper, *The Southern Workman*, in which he described the Indians' humanity and their love of Hampton Institute. Some of the articles contained notes written by Indian students after they had returned to their reservations, praising the school's teachers. At other times Washington could condescendingly write such things as, "The untutored Indian is anything but a graceful walker. Take off his moccasins and put shoes on him, and he does not know how to use his feet." In another article he wrote, "I think the true test of civilization in any race, is shown by the desire of that race to assist those whose position is more unfortunate than theirs. I do not mean to say that the Negro is thoroughly civilized, but I do mean it reflects much credit on his civilization to see him, while he himself is yet struggling for a place among civilized races, reaching out his hand to assist a less fortunate race." Washington believed that in helping the Indians he had demonstrated that he had risen above "mere race prejudices."

The story of what happened to the Indians that Washington taught is not as bright as he portrayed it in the school's newspaper. He apparently did not know the extent of misery that the Hampton experience caused some of the Indians. Stripped of their own culture, they were trained to act like the white man, only to return to reservations where they tried with difficulty and varying degrees of success to straddle two cultures. Washington never had any reason to stay in touch with his former students beyond the extent of publishing a few of their positive letters. The records of some of the Indians shows that a surprising number of them died young of various causes, some within a few years after leaving Hampton, most probably because of the harsh realities of reservation life.

Some of Washington's Indian students became teachers, others settled on farms. George Bushotter, a Dakota, went to work for the Smithsonian Institution and contributed numerous texts, in Dakota, on his own life and the customs and life of his people. Another, Thomas Wildcat Alford, a Shawnee, had been an interpreter at a Shawnee trading post before coming to Hampton. Perhaps more than any other Indian student of the time, he adopted the Hampton philosophy and worked to encourage the Shawnee to adopt the white man's ways. Eventually he became a large landowner during the Oklahoma land rush. The most accomplished of those who passed through Washington's Wigwam was James Murie, also known as Young Eagle, a Pawnee. At first a convert to the Hampton idea, Murie later came to appreciate his own culture still more. He became an accomplished writer and ethnologist on Pawnee culture, working at different times for the U.S. Bureau of American Ethnology and the Field Museum in Chicago.

At this point in his career Washington had established himself as a successful and versatile teacher and a prime product of Hampton Institute's philosophy of racial uplift through education (and indoctrination). He was an accomplished public speaker and a budding author whose articles, while filled with clichés and platitudes, always had a message of encouragement. Although he had not fully developed his own style of writing, he was doing better at shaping his message.

Washington's world was now about to change dramatically. In February 1881 the State of Alabama passed a law to establish a "Normal school [a school to train teachers, especially for the elementary grades] for colored teachers at Tuskegee." In May that year George Washington Campbell, an ex-slaveholder, banker, and leading citizen of Tuskegee wrote to General Armstrong on behalf of the Tuskegee trustees seeking his help in recommending a principal for the school. Armstrong replied, "The only man I can suggest is one Mr. Booker Washington, a graduate of this institution, a very competent capable mulatto, clear headed, modest, sensible, polite, and a thorough teacher and superior man. The best man we ever had here."

The Tuskegee trustees had expected Armstrong to recommend one of his white teachers. Time passed without a reply. Then one evening during chapel services, Armstrong was handed a telegram. When the service ended he rose and read the brief message to the assembled students, including Washington. It was from Tuskegee; it said that Booker Washington would suit them and to send him at once. The students and faculty burst into applause and shouts of joy. A black graduate of Hampton was about to become a school principal! It was a personal triumph for Washington and a validation of Hampton's success. The teacher of Indians was headed to a strange place with a Creek Indian name, in a state and county of which he knew nothing. He had no idea what his school looked like. What he did not know and was about to discover was that there was no school. It would be up to him to build one.

The town of Tuskegee could be found in Macon County, in southeastern Alabama, one of eleven counties that stretched across the southern part of the state, collectively known as the Black Belt for their rich black soil (and later for their high population percentages of African Americans). It was cotton country. The land around Tuskegee was the home of many former slaves who continued to plow the fields with their mules and work the cotton as freedmen. Washington discovered that the black cotton farmers and their families lived in primitive cabins where the whole family slept in one room and ate a diet consisting mainly of fat pork, cornbread, and black-eyed peas. It reminded him of his own circumstances as a slave on the Burroughs farm a generation earlier. Most of the black cotton farmers did not even have their own vegetable garden. Cotton often grew right up to the cabin walls. To have a garden plot sometimes meant negotiating with the landowner because it would mean less land for cotton, the money crop.

Macon was an extremely poor, predominantly black county in 1881, with almost 13,000 black residents and a white population of about 4,600. The town itself sat up on a slight hill. It was the county seat, with a population of about 2,000 people, almost evenly divided between white and black. The wealthy whites—the bankers, planters, and cotton brokers—lived in columned mansions and old plantation houses. Even though it was the county seat, the nearest railroad missed Tuskegee by five miles. Montgomery, the capital of Alabama, was forty miles west.

Washington was flabbergasted to find that there was no school. And no schoolbooks. And no place set aside to hold classes. Yet students of all ages were already clamoring to be enrolled. As he so often did in his public writing, he found something positive to say about his circumstances. In *Up from Slavery* he wrote, "Before going to Tuskegee I had expected to find there a building and all the necessary apparatus ready for me to begin teaching. To my disappointment, I found nothing of the kind. I did find, though, that which no costly building and apparatus can supply—hundreds of hungry, earnest souls who wanted to secure knowledge." The burning desire for education among so many blacks during Reconstruction continued unabated for generations after the Civil War. This movement to educate millions of former slaves had now reached Macon County, Alabama: the county had its first normal school, even if the classrooms themselves did not exist.

Undaunted, Washington set to work to build his school. His letters back to Hampton reveal that he wasted no time getting down to business. With one of the black trustees, Lewis Adams, he scouted the area for a site for the school. He found a hundred-acre farm with a few dilapidated build-

Washington as he appeared in 1881. He thought the mustache made him look older. *(Library of Congress)*

ings that he could purchase for $500. Washington wrote immediately to Hampton's treasurer, J. F. B. Marshall, and told him that the students could not afford to pay for their board and that he planned to use the "labor system" so they could work for it, just as Hampton students did. Washington asked Marshall for a loan of $200 to purchase the farm with the balance in installments at 8 percent interest. He would own the farm outright within a year.

The first reaction of George W. Campbell, Tuskegee's leading white citizen, upon meeting Washington was that he was much too young for such a position of responsibility. Campbell thought Washington looked to be only about eighteen years old. Actually he was twenty-five at the time and sported a bushy mustache, which he thought made him look older. It was Washington's businesslike manner, his focus, and his friendly demeanor, tempered with just the right amount of humility, that won over most local residents, white and black. He applied his philosophy to be "the force that wins." Within a month, thirty-seven students of both sexes ranging in age from sixteen to forty were enrolled at Tuskegee. Many others were turned away. Some of Washington's pupils were already teachers, but they knew that their rudimentary education made them barely more advanced than their students. Tuskegee would give them the training they needed to be real teachers.

Washington was a natural leader, and despite his youthful appearance he arrived in Tuskegee with the skills he needed to succeed. Although Macon County was a sea of black people with a few islands of whites, Washington realized that white people held the money and the political power locally and in the state. He would have to find ways to work within this reality if his school was to survive.

The school's very existence was due to the dedicated work of a prominent black resident, Lewis Adams, a former slave who was now a tinsmith and the most successful black merchant in Tuskegee. Adams taught Washington about local conditions in Macon County, and he learned that the creation of the normal school was the result of a political bargain. Black voters in the South were overwhelmingly Republican, the party of Abraham Lincoln who had freed the slaves. White Democratic office seekers in predominantly black areas like Macon County had to find ways to appeal to black voters. Alabama, like most other Southern states after the end of Reconstruction, was beginning the process of disfranchising black voters. But in 1880 the black vote still mattered. The white Democratic candidate for the state senate that year, Colonel Wilbur F. Foster, a Confederate veteran, struck a bargain with Lewis Adams. He asked Adams what it would take for him to deliver the black votes for his election. Adams wanted something for the black community in exchange; he wanted a normal school to train black teachers.

Democrats swept Alabama's elections in 1880, helped considerably by black voters, and Lewis Adams got his school. Washington read this as a sign that black voters were learning to "vote from principle" rather than by party. One black Macon Country resident told him that he always knew how to vote: first find out which way the white man is voting, then vote the other way. Washington, cautious as always in not wishing to offend white politicians, preferred to think that blacks should vote in the best interests of both races.

Local sentiment toward the new school for black teachers was one of skepticism tempered with political and economic necessity. Old attitudes of the former slavemasters died hard, or never died at all. Some former slaveowners, including the white chairman of the school's board of trustees, George Campbell, wondered why Negroes had to learn to read and write in the first place. There was concern too about a larger issue in Alabama: blacks were leaving the state in large numbers, many joining the Exoduster movement to Kansas in 1879. This not only hurt white business but threatened the steady supply of labor for the cotton fields. Merchants in Tuskegee had benefited from the dollars spent in their stores by white students from the local high school and also from the female college there. Perhaps the new normal school for blacks would help their business.

Washington discovered that the main reason many whites resented a black school was because an education might inspire blacks to move to towns and cities and seek a wider range of employment than was offered in the cotton fields of Macon County. A stereotype of an educated black man had grown up in the South, its origins pre–Civil War.

Washington described this character in *Up from Slavery* as a flashily dressed man in a "high hat, imitation gold eyeglasses, a showy walking cane, kid gloves, fancy boots, and what not—in a word, a man who was determined to live by his wits." Living by one's "wits" presumed something nefarious or illegal—in short, a confidence man rather than someone who sought an honest career.

Washington opened his school on July 4, 1881, in a shanty attached to a local African Methodist Episcopal church, until he could begin to fix up the farm. Soon several classes were moved to a henhouse and a stable on the farm property that would become Tuskegee Institute. Washington would later tell stories about the humble origins of his school, in which the henhouse figured prominently. The theme of his life's story was taking shape both in reality and as a self-made image of himself and his school that he would use with great skill to promote his work. In an era with a growing appreciation of stories about the lives of celebrities, Washington's career was beginning to take on mythic proportions. He became adept at cultivating his public image, at first innocently and subconsciously and later with deliberation and purpose as he became the most famous black man in America.

It would be hard to tell reality from the legend, so closely were the two intertwined in his public life. The fact that his best-selling autobiography, written twenty years after he opened Tuskegee Institute, would have the arresting title *Up from Slavery* was no accident. It captured the essence of post–Civil War America, where rags-to-riches stories saturated the entrepreneurial culture. *Up from Slavery* could have been the title of a book by Horatio Alger, Jr., one of the best-selling novelists of the time, who rivaled Mark Twain in popularity. Alger wrote more than 130 "dime novels," so called because they cost about ten cents each. These were adventure stories about ordinary people who were down on their luck or from humble backgrounds and discovered they could succeed in life through hard work and clean living. Alger wrote about Abraham Lincoln, who began as a lowly rail-splitter and rose to be president. He wrote about James A. Garfield, who ascended from canal worker to the nation's highest office. The story of Garfield's life appeared the same year that Washington launched Tuskegee Institute.

Washington's life was beginning to read like one of Alger's novels. He had risen from a slave boy to become a schoolteacher and eventually the principal of his own school. It helped the real story and the legendary aspects of it that he had begun his school under the most humble of circumstances—in a henhouse and a stable. Humble origins were important in an age when the nation was remaking itself and when immigrants like the steel magnate Andrew Carnegie had risen from poverty to vast wealth. It was the American dream: anyone who really tried could succeed. Washington and millions of others learned this from their blue-backed spellers, from Horatio Alger novels, and from many other popular sources that pushed the idea that anyone could succeed in America if only they tried hard and lived a moral life. With each new phase of Washington's career, the rise from slavery became more dramatic and more appealing as a sign of his personal success. More important, he was becoming a symbol of the success of his race.

In the midst of launching his school, Washington and Fanny Smith began their life together as they had dreamed of doing as soon as she was out of school. After Fanny graduated from Hampton in the spring of 1882, she and Washington returned to Malden that summer to be married by their hometown minister Reverend Rice at his Zion Baptist Church. They returned quickly to Tuskegee, where Fanny joined the faculty. They had little privacy in their all-to-brief marriage since most of the faculty lived together in a rented house. Fanny was the school's housekeeper, and the scant records of her life in Malden and at Tuskegee indicate that she was a hardworking, dedicated teacher, much in the mold of many Hampton graduates. She was responsible for developing a home economics program for the female students at the fledgling school.

In June 1883 the couple had a child, Portia, named for the character in Shakespeare's *Merchant of Venice*. Her middle name was Marshall, in honor of Hampton's treasurer who had been so kind to the father and mother, helping them through Hampton and lending money to build Tuskegee.

Less than a year later Fanny was taken ill and died at the age of twenty-six. Just what caused her death remains unknown. One story claims she fell from a wagon and suffered internal injuries; another suggests she had "consumption of the bowels." Baby Portia was cared for by nurses until Washington married again two years later.

There is little evidence in Washington's correspondence of how he handled his loss. But typical of his actions when faced with adversity throughout his life, he simply threw himself into his work with more determination. In one of the few references to Fanny's illness, written five days before she died, Washington wrote to his Hampton mentor General Armstrong, "The sickness of my wife caused me to have to leave Philadelphia when in the midst of success." Several years later he wrote briefly about her in a publication, "Her heart was set on making her home an object lesson for those about her, who were so much in need of such help."

In the fall of 1881 a new teacher came to Tuskegee Institute who would change Washington and the entire school. Five years later she would also become Washington's second wife. Olivia A. Davidson had been born in 1854 in Virginia and was probably the mulatto child listed among the slaves

Olivia Davidson, whom Washington married in 1886, became his second wife and a major influence on the early development of Tuskegee Institute. *(Henry Whittemore Library, Framingham State College)*

of James C. Davidson in Tazewell County. After the Civil War she traveled with her family to Albany, Ohio, where she was educated in the public schools and became a school-teacher. Albany had been a destination for slaves after the war. The Albany Enterprise Academy, a black-owned and operated school, attracted many newly freed slaves seeking an education.

Olivia Davidson's story rivals that of Booker Washington. Taken together they embodied much of the Reconstruction and post-Reconstruction struggle to educate blacks in the South. In the 1870s Davidson went to Hernando, Mississippi, with her brother Joseph to teach in a freedmen's school. When her brother was murdered, reportedly by the Ku Klux Klan, she moved to Memphis to teach until a yellow fever epidemic closed that school. She then studied at Hampton Institute for two years, graduating in 1879, her tuition having been paid by Mrs. Rutherford B. Hayes, a prominent Ohioan and wife of the president. Davidson had not been happy with the level of education at Hampton and hoped for something better. With help from a white philanthropist, Mary Hemenway, she spent two years at Framingham State Normal School in Massachusetts before moving to Tuskegee.

Olivia Davidson was a woman with a strong sense of social responsibility. While her health was never robust, she nonetheless threw herself into her work at Tuskegee Institute. She was better educated than Washington, and an examination of his speeches and letters after her arrival shows a trend toward more literary references and other refinements that were missing from his earlier writings. Five years after her arrival at Tuskegee, and two years after the death of Washington's first wife, he married Olivia in an Ohio wedding in 1886. She was Washington's partner in the growth of Tuskegee Institute as lady principal, as well as a partner in marriage. She raised Washington's daughter, Portia, from his first marriage, and bore two sons, Booker T. Washington, Jr., and Ernest Davidson Washington.

In 1889, after a fire at the Washington home, Olivia's long-standing respiratory ailments worsened. She received care from the family doctor, C. N. Dorsette, and a nurse who was sent from Boston. As her condition worsened she was sent to Massachusetts General Hospital in Boston, where she died on May 9. At age thirty-three, Washington was a widower for the second time. He was stunned by Olivia's passing, and it took many years for him to get over her death. She was the love of his life and his partner in building Tuskegee.

Olivia Davidson Washington had as much to do with the success of Tuskegee in its founding years as her husband did. In his first autobiography, *The Story of My Life and Work*, Booker acknowledged that the very existence of the school was "due more to Miss Davidson than any one else." She was a tireless fund-raiser for the institution and regularly made visits to white and black families around Tuskegee seeking support in any amount, large or small. Fairs and festivals on campus sometimes netted donations in the form of a hog or a chicken.

Olivia Washington's greatest success as a fund-raiser was in New England, where her contacts helped open the purses of Northern philanthropists who supported black education in the South. She was especially effective in convincing New England women to support the school. Olivia wrote many letters to New England donors asking for money, schoolbooks, clothing, equipment, and anything that would further Tuskegee's mission. She traveled north to plead for donations, appearing at Sunday schools and other church meetings and visiting the homes of potential donors. Once she met a woman on a boat while they were sailing to New England and managed to get a fifty-dollar donation on the spot. After Olivia's death, Washington followed in her footsteps, making regular fund-raising tours of New England for the rest of his life.

The other great force that made Tuskegee a success was the students themselves. The sweat equity they put into the campus made the difference. Tuskegee Institute was virtually built by the students, brick by brick. This was the labor system Washington had learned at Hampton—students earned tuition and board by working. Washington tirelessly reminded potential donors that their money would be used

Students at Tuskegee Institute, ca. 1900, built their school brick by brick. *(Library of Congress)*

to make black students self-sufficient wage earners. Just weeks after his marriage to Olivia, he delivered a fund-raising speech before the Unitarian National Conference in Saratoga, New York, titled "Our Opportunity Through the South," in which he laid out the Tuskegee plan to his Northern audience. Tuskegee Institute, he told the Unitarians, had a farm, a blacksmith shop, a brickyard, a sawmill, a printing office, and a "girls' sewing room, laundry, and cooking class," all of which taught students practical skills that would get them jobs and prepare them to teach others to do the same. Student labor in these shops and sewing rooms would build the school and teach students how to help themselves. Nothing resonated better with audiences north or south, black or white, than the idea of self-help. In America, people could lift themselves up by their own boot-straps, and everyone believed that God helps those who help themselves. It was a formula for success.

Tuskegee Institute grew steadily in its early years. The student body doubled to sixty-six in the second year. Student workers completed Porter Hall, the first brick building on campus, a three-story structure that housed classrooms and offices. The building was named for a Brooklyn white man, A. H. Porter, who donated money toward its erection. Tuskegee's success soon began to draw the attention of wider audiences, especially in the North, and also because it was an offshoot of Hampton, a well-known commodity to those who followed black education in the South. Booker T. Washington's mentor, Samuel Chapman Armstrong, and others at Hampton, especially Hampton's treasurer, J. F. B. Marshall, continued to find ways to support Tuskegee Institute and sing its praises in ever widening circles of educators and donors.

Washington's work at Tuskegee came to be seen as a prime example of "industrial education," the educational theory then in vogue in the United States and other parts of the industrial world. Washington did not invent this idea, nor did Samuel Chapman Armstrong at Hampton Institute. Its roots lay in the views of some educators before the Civil War who looked for a way to make education more practical and disciplined. After the war the idea of industrial education caught on as a movement affecting both white and black students. It seemed to be appropriate for unskilled immigrants who were coming to America's shores as well as for former slaves.

Hampton and Tuskegee became models of industrial education for blacks in the South. During Reconstruction the Freedmen's Bureau and its missionary school supporters encouraged the creation of manual labor schools which fit the industrial education movement. Many missionary school workers, especially those with military backgrounds such as Samuel Chapman Armstrong, saw industrial education in terms of a moral movement. Hard work, discipline, and Christianity went hand in hand for the betterment of all. While some educators believed that manual training was primarily a tool for discipline, others saw the urgent need to train a reliable and skilled class of workers to meet the needs of expanding factories and industries. Still others included the idea of scientific farming under the rubric of "industrial." Hundreds of schools placed the word "industrial" or "polytechnic" in their names and practiced varying degrees of the industrial education idea. Tuskegee began as the Tuskegee Normal School, but it was not long before its full name was the Tuskegee Normal and Industrial Institute.

Washington's own views of industrial education were clearly stated in a speech he gave before the Alabama State Teachers' Association in 1882. He told the teachers at the convention,

> I shall speak, for a few minutes, of Industrial Education, mainly as it relates to the colored people at the present time. I think that three distinct advantages may be claimed for such an education. First—Under wise management it aids students in securing mental training; secondly, it teaches him how to earn a living; and thirdly, it teaches him the dignity of labor.

Industrial education, Washington said, was the only way most black students could afford any kind of education. They did not have the money for tuition or board unless they worked for it. Washington's views were based on what he had learned at Hampton and the world he had discovered in Macon County, Alabama. Education was useless unless it helped students find employment, he thought. Describing conditions faced by the masses of blacks in the South, he observed:

> View, for a moment four millions of people plodding on, from year to year, without homes, and with no plan or system for

work, but merely dragging out an existence. Their sons are growing up without trades, and their daughters with no idea of household economy. Such a glance must give one an idea of the importance of industrial education.

Washington's early educational experience had freed him from ignorance and started him on the path of personal freedom, but it was not industrial education. He experienced the broad movement of universal education spawned in large part by the freedmen. Most newly freed slaves equated education with emancipation. This included higher education for those who could get it and, in general, a broad, liberal definition of education modeled after typical schools for whites in New England and elsewhere. In the United States education had long been tied to the idea of democracy, citizenship, and freedom. Washington had internalized this vision of education from his Webster's blue-black speller. But once he discovered industrial education at Hampton and became one of its chief disciples, his focus on industrial education overshadowed any idea of education as a goal in itself, as part of being a free citizen in a democracy. Industrial education in many ways subverted the earlier black universal education movement in the South, according to James D. Anderson, a leading scholar of black education in the South. Industrial education may have fit the needs of the times, but its critics, then and later, would argue that Washington's constant promotion of industrial education came at a price to those who sought a broader concept that included higher education and a curriculum with less emphasis on developing job skills.

While not all black schools in the South embraced industrial education, it was extensive. In Atlanta, for example, five black colleges and a black theological seminary were operating at the time Washington was building Tuskegee Institute. Atlanta Baptist College (later Morehouse College and then Morehouse University) did not offer trades as part of its curriculum until the 1890s. Its counterpart womens' school, Atlanta Baptist Female Seminary (later Spelman College), offered nursing and domestic economy classes. Nearby Clark University had a full program of industrial education for men, including carpentry, blacksmithing, and basic engineering. Clark's extensive machine shops boasted lathes for woodworking, drill presses, and Goodyear shoemaking machinery. Women at Clark could take sewing and dressmaking.

There were compelling practical reasons for black schools to build their programs on the industrial education model. In the increasingly hostile racial environment of the South, industrial education offered a compromise that whites and blacks could accept. Northern white philanthropists saw it as a means to lift a race out of slavery and make productive, moral citizens. Southerners, who had earlier opposed carpetbaggers in the Freedmen's Bureau for meddling in Southern affairs, and who had opposed black education as unnecessary, came to understand that industrial education was a safe and practical solution to the need for black labor in the South. Industrial education could produce workers who would cast down their buckets in the rural South. The money from white philanthropists brought goodwill and much needed capital as it fueled the industrial education movement at Tuskegee and at many other black schools in the South.

Without the infusion of money from white philanthropists, many of the schools could not have survived. The Peabody Fund, begun in 1867 by George Peabody, a successful Massachusetts-born merchant, pumped $2 million into black education, mostly for primary schooling, before it went out of business in 1898. The John F. Slater Fund, begun in 1882, gave a million dollars to black industrial education and prompted Congress to strike a gold medal for Slater's efforts to uplift a race. Later, in 1901, the Southern Education Board would consolidate many education philanthropists into a national board. Even black intellectuals and supporters of black higher education, like Harvard-trained W. E. B. Du Bois, looked with favor on the work of the Slater Fund to promote industrial education. Du Bois wrote in 1902, "Perhaps the greatest single impulse toward the economic emancipation of the Negro has been the singularly wise administration of the John F. Slater Fund."

CHAPTER FOUR

The Beginning of an Era

Though we are not yet where we want to be, yet, thank God, we are not where we used to be.—Booker T. Washington, *September* 20, 1895

In 1892, Washington married for the third time. Just as he had done in his previous marriages, he chose another Tuskegee faculty member for his bride. Margaret James Murray may never have replaced Olivia as the true love of Washington's life, but she brought many important elements and stabilizing influences. Maggie, as she was often called, had been born of a black mother and an Irish immigrant father in Mississippi, probably about 1861. She may have lied about her age to enter Fisk University's preparatory classes in 1881 by claiming she was four years younger, stating her birth date as 1865. She completed the preparatory classes and the regular curriculum at Fisk in 1889 and joined the Tuskegee faculty that year. One of her classmates at Fisk was W. E. B. Du Bois, and they remained friends despite the rift that would grow between Washington and Du Bois in the years ahead.

Maggie, like Olivia before her, became lady principal of Tuskegee in 1890, the year she began a courtship with Washington that led to marriage. She was an attractive woman, lighter in color than her husband—as lovely as a Gibson girl, the model of feminine beauty in the 1890s, except "her hair

Margaret James Murray (ca. 1900), Washington's third wife, was lady principal at Tuskegee and a leader in the black women's club movement. *(Library of Congress)*

is kinky," one white observer described her. Photographs reveal her as a proper Victorian woman in dress and comportment, slightly plump but without a doubt handsome. She served in a number of important capacities at Tuskegee, especially related to the female students, and was hostess for Washington's burgeoning social life that involved prominent visitors who needed to be properly attended. She also took command of Washington's three children, though it is not clear how they took to their new stepmother. She and Washington would have no children of their own. She also became a prominent club woman who in 1895 was elected

Washington's family ca. 1899. From left, E. Davidson, Booker T. Jr., Margaret, Washington, and Portia. *(National Park Service)*

president of the National Association of Colored Women's Clubs, the segregated counterpart of the white women's club movement.

The correspondence between Booker and Maggie rarely contains signs of personal affection, but this may be because most of what survives often relates to the school and its workings. Even though they lived and worked on campus together, Washington would send her notes—interoffice memos of sorts—about business and personal matters. Once he wrote and asked her to take a carriage ride with him, but she replied that she was not up to going behind those horses. She carved out a number of areas for herself and made the most of being one of the inner circle of administrators that ran Tuskegee Institute.

In the last week of August 1895, Washington received an invitation to speak at the opening ceremonies of the Cotton States and International Exposition in Atlanta. This great event was to be the South's answer to the spectacularly successful World's Columbian Exposition, held two years earlier in Chicago. It was a singular opportunity for Washington to reach a large audience of prominent white people with his message of how best to achieve race progress in America. He was excited by the prospect, quickly accepted the offer, and began immediately to write his remarks.

The Cotton States and International Exposition was scheduled to open September 18, so Washington had fewer than three weeks to prepare. But in reality his entire career to this point had readied him for the task ahead. What Washington could not anticipate was the effect that this single speech would have on his life. It would thrust him into national and international prominence more than anything else he would ever say or do. Time and circumstances were coming together in such a way that Booker T. Washington would quickly become the most famous black person in the world and the most powerful race leader in the United States. He had worked hard and followed a careful strategy to secure the invitation to speak at Atlanta. It did not arrive by chance.

Washington had already spent fourteen years building Tuskegee Institute, and in the process he had become a well-known educator in the South. He traveled regularly to New England and the Midwest to raise money for his school. He had a reputation as an excellent speaker, something he had been cultivating for more than twenty years, since his first youthful forays into public speaking in Malden, West Virginia. In his autobiography he expresses humility about his public speaking, saying he did not set out to become a speaker and that he would rather be doing other things than talking about what he did. But despite his public modesty on the subject, he knew that his talent served him well before all audiences.

Washington was an entertaining storyteller who knew how to reach people and get his point across. He spoke crisply and distinctly with very little accent when speaking in public, but he could disarm his listeners by telling jokes in Negro dialect, proving he could make fun of himself and his race. This worked with white and black audiences, though many better-educated blacks cringed when Washington took this path. He was fond of telling chicken jokes, where the chickens were "gathered from miscellaneous sources," a reference to slave days when slaves would steal chickens from their masters.

In an era before radio or electronic amplification, oratory, both indoors and outdoors, was a major source of entertainment, inspiration, and information for millions of Americans who were quite willing to sit or stand for long periods of time to hear an interesting speech. As Tuskegee Institute developed, Washington sought financial support from prominent white philanthropists and furthered his own popularity among some of the leading industrialists and most influential businessmen in the country. These important backers were among his greatest promoters for speaking engagements.

Through his wealthy friends, Washington reached Northern white audiences early in his career. This new invitation to speak in Atlanta gave him the opportunity to speak before a largely white audience of prominent Southerners, a group that Washington desperately wanted to reach. His work was in the South, and the great bulk of the black population lived in the South. It was the white South that Washington had to win over if his work was to expand and flourish. He had worked diligently for this opportunity for a number of years.

He was fond of telling how two years earlier, in 1893, he had traveled two thousand miles to give a five-minute speech just so he could get his message to an audience of Southern whites.

At the time, in November 1893, he had been on a speaking and fund-raising mission in Boston when an offer came to speak before an international meeting of Christian workers in Atlanta. Washington boarded a train in Boston, traveled to Atlanta, gave his five-minute talk, and then an hour later boarded the train back to Boston. He spoke before a convention of two thousand people. Exactly what he said that day is not known; no copy of his speech has ever been found. But it is clear from newspaper accounts that he talked about his work at Tuskegee and the school's growth, and how the black man was helping himself by acquiring an education, learning a craft, and getting a job. He talked about the importance of industrial education, and, since this was a religious gathering, he noted the need for religious and academic training. This was his usual message, and in five minutes it was about all he could say.

Perhaps as important as what Washington said was his demeanor and what he didn't say that caught the attention of the largely white audience and a smaller segregated section of blacks to whom he spoke. The influential *Atlanta Journal* printed a story about the opening of the Christian workers convention on the day Washington spoke. "The eyes of the delegates to the Christian workers convention were opened by a colored man this morning," the *Journal* reported. "He gave a plain and simple but very intelligent account of a great work being done among the colored people—an account that was worth more than a cart load of the gush some of the delegates have been getting off on the negro question about which they know as much as a 'hog knows about holiday.'"

The *Journal* praised Washington though earlier it had attacked other black participants at the convention. Two days before he spoke, the same newspaper printed a story with the headline "Drawing the Color Line/ Some 'Uppity' Darkeys Have Wounded Feelings/ With Their Noses in the Air They Leave the Convention." Before Washington arrived, about a dozen black delegates had protested the segregated seating arrangement at the gathering after one black man had taken a seat in the white section, only to be removed by police. The *Journal* criticized the black delegates for listening to some of the white speakers who were arguing for social equality. It was not lost on Atlanta's white establishment that Booker T. Washington seemed to be a safe speaker who talked of uplift without agitating for social equality.

The next year Washington was invited to be part of a delegation of prominent Atlanta whites, including the mayor, a former governor, a newspaper editor, and wealthy businessmen and cotton merchants, who went to Washington, D.C., to lobby Congress for an appropriation to defray expenses of the Cotton States and International Exposition. Two other black men, both prominent bishops—Abram L. Grant of Texas and Wesley J. Gaines of Georgia—were also in the delegation.

Washington had been in the nation's capital before, but never to visit Capitol Hill, and never to speak before a committee of Congress. In the course of his visit he managed to meet prominent politicians, including the speaker of the House, Charles Crisp of Georgia, and Thomas Brackett Reed of Maine, the former speaker who would soon be speaker again. He clearly enjoyed being around these politicians and being included in the delegation with prominent Southerners.

For two hours the white delegates testified before the committee's packed hearing room. Finally the three black members of the delegation were allowed to speak. All three testified that the Atlanta Exposition would be a good showcase for race progress in the South. Washington spoke last and for almost twenty minutes, despite the fact that the time allotted for the hearing was almost over. What he said foreshadowed his address the following year at the exposition. He tells the story of his testimony in his autobiography:

> . . . I tried to impress upon the committee, with all the earnestness and plainness of any language that I could command, that if Congress wanted to do something which would assist in ridding the South of the race question and making friends between the two races, it should, in every proper way, encourage the material and intellectual growth of both races.

He said the exposition would show the world what both races had accomplished since the days of slavery. Then he uttered the heart of his message, which would be honed and polished by the time of the exposition, when he told the House Committee on Appropriations that "while the Negro should not be deprived by unfair means of the franchise, political agitation alone would not save him, and that back of the ballot he must have property, industry, skill, economy, intelligence, and character, and that no race without these elements could permanently succeed."

He reminded the congressmen that he had always steered clear of politics and had agreed to join the delegation only because he thought the exposition would give his race an opportunity to show what it had accomplished. Here he was, a rare black lobbyist in one of the nation's highest political forums, working side by side with white politicians yet claiming that he usually stayed out of politics. He put himself forward as a compromiser and a reconciler, not an agitator. He was there not to demand anything but to be helpful to whites while speaking on behalf of the black South. This strategy worked so well for him that he adhered to it the rest of his life. It would give him more power than any black man in America had ever had.

The Atlanta delegation commended Washington for his support and for his remarks. Once the appropriation bill passed and the exposition was under way, its white planners offered Washington the opportunity to oversee the creation of a separate Negro Building that was to be a feature of the event. Some blacks in Atlanta had protested the creation of a Negro Building as a further sign of racial segregation in the South. Many recalled the fiasco the year before at the Columbian Exposition in Chicago, where Negro Day featured truckloads of watermelons brought in to please black patrons—a display of racial insensitivity that seemed totally lost on the white planners.

Washington did not object to a separate Negro Building. He saw it not as a matter of racial segregation but as an opportunity to demonstrate what blacks had accomplished. The building was to be built by black tradesmen and managed by blacks, and would showcase black progress. Washington's own school was such a place—built by blacks, run by blacks, and a demonstration of black progress. His alma mater, Hampton Institute, and his own school, Tuskegee Institute, would have prominent exhibits in the Negro Building. It offered too many benefits; there was no time to worry about the symbols of segregation. Nevertheless Washington turned down the job of managing the Negro Building because of his responsibilities at Tuskegee. He recommended another black, I. Garland Penn of Virginia, to direct the Negro Department of the Exposition.

Washington was appointed one of five black Alabama commissioners to the Negro Department. Later Penn would urge the white commissioners to invite Washington to give an opening-day address. The commissioners, led by the exposition's president, Charles A. Collier, at first wanted him to speak on the occasion of the opening of the Negro Building. But Penn saw this as an affront to Washington and a potential setback for race progress. He worked tirelessly behind the scenes to secure Washington a place at the main ceremony for the opening of the exposition.

When the invitation to Washington was finally extended, it was news throughout the South. The *Atlanta Constitution* announced that "A Colored Orator Has Been Invited to Participate in the Opening." Exposition officials felt the need to explain their actions by calling Washington a "strong personality" who had done great work for the exposition with his testimony before Congress. Penn sent Washington the newspaper clipping and wrote: "You are the man."

Black newspapers picked up the story and took heart in the fact that a major Southern exposition would showcase black progress and feature a black man as one of its opening speakers. The *Washington Colored American* observed that the Atlanta Exposition "has shown a disposition all along to treat the colored brother with that consideration which his worth deserves. It has given him just what he has been asking for since emancipation, namely, an opportunity to show what he is capable of doing." The newspaper added, ". . . every colored woman, man, and child who can possibly get there ought to go, if for no other reason than to hold up the hands of Prof. Washington, as the children of Israel held up the arms of Moses while he fought the battles of the Lord." Even before his famous speech, Washington found himself cast in the role of Moses.

Washington's friends and supporters looked forward to this speech with great anticipation and no small degree of anxiety. Robert C. Bedford, a white minister who had founded a black Congregational church in Montgomery,

Alabama, and who served as secretary of Tuskegee's board of trustees, wrote to Washington, "I think the matter of your speaking at the opening of the Exposition is one of the greatest land marks in the history of freedom. It will receive universal comment on both sides [of] the sea." But as the day of the speech approached, Washington worried that even though he was well prepared, the occasion was fraught with great peril. The white South would be listening; the whole country would be listening. He wrote several drafts of the speech, crossing out passages and reworking them. He practiced reading the speech to his wife Margaret and, two days before his delivery in Atlanta, before the entire Tuskegee faculty. He worked on the cadence of the speech, on shifting gears between big ideas and telling entertaining stories with a moral.

Washington had to find a way to reach three distinct audiences: Northern whites, Southern whites, and blacks. Within each of these groups there was disagreement about the best road to race progress and race harmony in America. Yet those who gave the subject much thought, black or white, yearned for an end to the burdens that slavery had imposed on America since the birth of the nation. The generation that fought the Civil War, Yankees and Confederates alike, would be listening to Washington's speech. So too would those who had lived through Reconstruction, with its temporary burst of freedom and equality for blacks that had been shattered by the terrorism of the Ku Klux Klan. Both former Klansmen and former abolitionists would be in the audience. The slaves who were freed by the war but found that freedom did not come easy would also be listening. And so would some of their former owners.

Most of white America, North and South, continued to harbor deep-seated notions that blacks were an inferior race. Racial segregation was growing, especially in the South.

Race violence in the form of lynching and political intimidation had not abated in the nearly twenty years since the end of Reconstruction. In the 1890s Southern state constitutions were building race barriers, not tearing them down. White politicians were still being elected by promising to keep blacks "in their place" as second-class citizens.

Throughout the agricultural South millions of blacks eked out a living as sharecroppers, bound to the land and their white landowners with seemingly no way out of a system that could be as pernicious as slavery. Those who worked in industry were often confined to the lowest-paid manual labor, and those in the trades were often denied access to unions. Only in a few industries, such as coal mining or bricklaying, did blacks fare about as well as whites in the same jobs.

The South was economically depressed in 1895, still feeling the effects of the Panic of 1893, which saw thousands of business failures across the nation, including major railroads and banks. It was doubly hard for blacks to get an economic leg up with the economy so weak and with black jobs threatened by vast numbers of white immigrants who were flooding into the country in unprecedented numbers.

On the day of Washington's speech the weather was clear and hot. A long procession of dignitaries, officials, and marching units, both white and black, made its way to the fairgrounds for opening-day ceremonies. The fact that black military units had a place in the procession with white units was a remarkable feature of the parade. This long procession, in stifling heat, along streets filled with American flags, took almost three hours. This only added to Washington's apprehension. He later wrote, ". . . when I got to the Exposition I felt rather fagged out, and very much feared that my address was going to prove a complete failure."

The heat inside the building offered no relief. He found the auditorium packed to the rafters while thousands more milled about outside unable to get in. Blacks who were fortunate enough to gain admission sat in a segregated section. Only two black people mounted the stage with the white dignitaries, Washington and I. Garland Penn of the Negro Department. As Washington crossed the stage to take his seat, a cheer went up from those in the Jim Crow seats.

Outside the auditorium was a prominent white man who could have entered but was too nervous to do so. William H. Baldwin, Jr., vice president and general manager of the Southern Railroad, was one of Washington's staunchest white friends and a trustee of Tuskegee Institute. A descendant of abolitionists, Baldwin was as worried as Washington about the reception to the speech. He could not bear to witness it; he paced around the outside of the building until the ceremony was over. As a major industrialist, Baldwin saw the racial climate in the South as a serious impediment to the industrial development of the region. He had firsthand experience as the employer of thousands of blacks on the Southern Railroad, and he feared potential clashes between white and black workers. Baldwin believed that a race war was a real possibility in the South.

Inside the auditorium the speeches began, with former Alabama governor Rufus Bullock as master of ceremonies. Between speeches Victor Herbert conducted the popular Gilmore's Band, which entertained the audience. The speaker just before Washington was a prominent white Atlanta socialite, Mrs. Joseph Thompson (Emma Mims Thompson), who headed the Woman's Department of the exposition. Newspaper accounts described her as "tall, slender, beautiful," her face covered with a white veil. She nervously read her speech from the podium with a thin voice that could scarcely be heard ten feet away.

Finally, in late afternoon, with the sun's rays streaming through the windows and onto the stage, it was Washington's turn. Newspaper reporters from the North and South picked up their attention—they had been waiting for the moment. They knew that a black man speaking to a largely white audience in the South would be news. President Grover Cleveland had pushed a button from his summer White House on Cape Cod to launch the machinery of the exposition, but what was about to happen would be the lead story, one way or another. After Emma Thompson sat down, the band played a medley of tunes, and then the audience grew silent in anticipation. Governor Bullock rose to introduce Washington by saying, "We shall now be favored with an address by a great Southern educator." This was greeted with general applause until Washington stood, whereupon the audience grew deathly quiet, as if it did not know quite how to act at this moment. Bullock continued, "We have with us today a representative of Negro enterprise and Negro civilization." It seemed proper to applaud again: Washington was back in his place as a Negro. The Jim Crow section had no trouble cheering and hollering, their applause noticeably louder than that from the vastly larger number of whites in the audience.

It was a short speech, fewer than sixteen hundred words, and probably took eight or nine minutes to deliver. As Washington moved to the center of the stage, the sunlight was directly in his face, lighting him dramatically, adding a warm reddish glow to his light-brown skin and causing his steel-grey eyes to shine with laser intensity. He was not a tall man—a muscular 5 feet 9 nine inches—but he seemed taller to the audience that day. One reporter said he was "a remarkable figure, tall, bony, straight as a Sioux chief, high forehead, straight nose, heavy jaws, and strong, determined mouth, with big white teeth, piercing eyes and a commanding manner."

Washington spent a few seconds determining whether or not he could avoid staring into the sunlight, but he quickly decided to look straight into it. He planted his feet with his heels together and his toes spread as if standing at attention, and, holding a pencil in one hand, the nonthreatening symbol of an educator, the tool of his trade, he began to speak in a resoundingly clear voice that could be heard all through the building.

He began by reminding his audience that one-third of the population of the South "is of the Negro race," and that anyone seeking to improve the "material, civil, or moral welfare of this section" could not ignore this black presence. He thanked the managers of the exposition for the great opportunity to showcase race progress and for their generosity. With these preliminaries out of the way, he turned to a history lesson that he knew would be popular with white Southerners. Washington was not merely trying to please the whites in the audience. He too believed, as did his mentor General Armstrong, that black political agitation was not the answer to race progress. Referring to his own generation of newly freed slaves as "ignorant and inexperienced," he observed that it was not surprising that blacks had turned first to politics after gaining their freedom. The freed slaves began their new lives "at the top instead of the bottom; that a seat in Congress or the state legislature was more sought than real estate or industrial skill; that the political convention or stump speaking had more attractions than starting a dairy farm or truck garden."

In just a few sentences Washington summarized and affirmed the white view of the failure of Reconstruction—that the bottom rung was on top. The newly freed slaves had gained political office and political power before they were ready for it—this is what the white South believed. Some blacks, including Washington, also doubted the success of the brief heyday of black officeholders. At the time Washington delivered this speech, most of the black politicians of the Reconstruction Era had been driven from office as white Redeemers reclaimed the political power they considered rightfully theirs. Even more telling was the fact that blacks had been steadily disfranchised in the 1880s and 1890s, to the point where political participation at any level in the South had virtually been denied to them.

Washington's acceptance of the white view of Reconstruction was meant to disarm his critics in the audience that day. It was the strategy of a compromiser. He did not bring up history to complain of past injustice; he used history to explain the present situation in a way that whites in the audience would find acceptable. He had to win them over before he could tell them what needed to be done.

Washington now shifted gears to tell a story about a ship lost at sea without fresh water. When the ship finally encountered another vessel, the captain of the distressed ship begged for water. The other ship's captain told him to "Cast down your bucket where you are." It turned out that the two ships were at the mouth of the Amazon River, and the water beneath them was not salt water but fresh water. The moral of the story was that blacks should cast down their buckets in the South rather than seeking a better life somewhere else. They should cultivate friendships with their white neighbors. They should cast their buckets in Southern agriculture and commerce, domestic service, and the professions. "It is at the bottom of life that we must begin, and not at the top," Washington said. "Nor should we permit our grievances to overshadow our opportunities." He was making peace with the white South because he saw reconciliation in the acceptance of things as they were. Realistically he recognized that whites held political, economic, and social power in the South as well as the nation. He was after a piece of it—the piece he thought he could claim at that time, in that place.

Washington attempted to address the labor situation in a manner that would benefit blacks. He understood that blacks were competing with immigrant labor. If blacks left the South, they would find even stiffer opposition in the North, where trade unions denied blacks an equal chance to work. He thought the best chance for a black man or woman to find a job was in the South, and then to hold on to those jobs that were traditionally theirs.

He then asked whites to cast down their buckets "among the eight millions of Negroes whose habits you know, whose fidelity and love you have tested in days when to have proved treacherous meant the ruin of your firesides." He appealed to another part of Southern legend, memory, and history by referring to the loyalty of many slaves to their masters during the Civil War. He spoke of the complex ties between blacks and whites, albeit as slave and master. Blacks, he said, would be better laborers for the South than all the foreign immigrants who were pouring into the country at the time. Many businessmen in the South were wary of the new immigrants, and Washington played on that suspicion by offering black laborers as the familiar labor pool.

The heart of Washington's speech was his offer of a racial bargain, a compromise that he thought might begin the end of the terrible racial tensions in America. He reiterated the offer several times during the speech: he accepted social segregation of the races as long as blacks would have opportunities for economic advancement. He called for an end to agitation for civil rights and political activism if blacks would be free to get an education, find a job, and earn a dollar. Thrusting his left hand high into the air where it stood out dramatically in the strong sunlight, Washington held his five fingers wide apart and said: "In all things that are purely social we can be as separate as the fingers," then he quickly closed them into a fist, almost as a salute, and said, "yet one as the hand in all things essential to mutual progress." The audience responded with thunderous applause and cheers. He followed this idea with another:

> The wisest among my race understand that the agitation of questions of social equality is the extremest folly, and that progress in the enjoyment of privileges that will come to us must be the result of severe and constant struggle rather than artificial forcing. . . . The opportunity to earn a dollar in a factory just now is worth infinitely more than the opportunity to spend a dollar in an opera-house.

He concluded with an emotional appeal pledging the support of his race above all else in solving the "intricate problem which God has laid at the doors of the South," so that sectional differences and racial animosities could fall away to absolute justice for all. "This, coupled with our material prosperity, will bring into our beloved South a new heaven and a new earth." He concluded this entirely secular speech with a powerful Christian image—a vision from the Book of Revelation itself.

Washington did not even have time to get back to his seat before the assembly of whites and blacks, male and female, young and old, former slaves and former masters, white politicians, industrialists, and seasoned reporters broke into wild and delirious applause. Hats flew through the air; a sea of waving handkerchiefs appeared; people of both races cried openly. Never in the history of the nation had a black speaker so thoroughly won over practically everyone who heard him, regardless of race, creed, or color. Governor Bullock leaped out of his seat, ran to Washington and shook his hand. A few minutes of oratory seemed to have launched a new beginning in race relations for the South.

Washington was not the last speaker on the program. In fact the main speaker of the day, Judge Emory Speer, a former member of Congress from Georgia, had the great misfortune to follow Washington's remarks. By the time he finished the sun was out of the sky and the auditorium was filled with shadows and gloom. No one gave his speech a second thought. Washington had not only stolen the show, he had articulated better than anyone before him a plan that seemed to offer hope and racial peace. The South and the rest of the nation seemed ready to embrace the racial strategy of the man from Tuskegee.

Reporters wasted no time telegraphing their glowing stories to newspapers across the country and around the world. One of the leading journalists of the time, James Creelman of the *New York World*, wrote a long, detailed account of the speech that remains one of the best eyewitness reports. The multiple headlines of his story included such lines as "SOUTH'S NEW EPOCH"; "A NEGRO MOSES SPOKE FOR A RACE," and "Booker T. Washington's Consummate Plea Made Him the Hero of the Occasion." Creelman reported that Clark Howell, a leading spokesmen for the New South, told him, "That man's speech is the beginning of a moral revolution in America."

Washington responded to Creelman's story the next day by sending a letter to the editor of the *New York World*. He was clearly in a state of euphoria, but he tempered his great moment with humility. What transpired at the exposition, he wrote, "was the brightest, most hopeful day in the history of the negro race." "I had no dream," he continued, "that any colored man thirty years after slavery could be received and treated in Atlanta with such distinction and honor." Lest he seem to be boasting he added, "I care nothing for the personal commendation. It is the race that I speak for. This is the year of jubilee of the negro. It is the beginning of an era."

For weeks afterward, Washington received telegrams and letters of congratulation from friends and total strangers—

whites and blacks, ex-Confederates and ex-Union soldiers across the country. He won universal praise in the most superlative terms. One letter came from W. E. B. Du Bois, the black intellectual and academician who would later become one of Washington's sharpest critics. But in September 1895 Du Bois wrote: "My Dear Mr. Washington: Let me heartily congratulate you upon your phenomenal success at Atlanta—it was a word fitly spoken." Du Bois also wrote to the black newspaper the *New York Age* that Washington's speech "might be the basis of a real settlement between whites and blacks in the South."

While Washington rode high on a wave of instant fame and almost universal acceptance as the leading spokesman for his race, a small but significant occurrence highlighted for him how far both he and his race had yet to travel. The day after the Atlanta speech, one of Washington's teachers, Robert W. Taylor, was assigned the task of accompanying Washington's daughter Portia on a train trip from Atlanta to Framingham, Massachusetts. They traveled on the Southern Railroad, a line managed by Tuskegee trustee William Baldwin. The station agent was aware that his boss expected Booker T. Washington's daughter and her companion to receive respectful treatment—but no one bothered to tell the conductor.

Taylor and Portia sat in seats facing each other until the white conductor came into the car to punch their tickets and ordered Taylor to turn the seat around and face forward. Taylor said he preferred riding backward. This irritated the conductor, who grabbed Taylor by his vest, tearing off three buttons. Taylor tried to fend off the conductor, who then hit Taylor in the mouth with his fist that held the ticket punch. The blow caused a severe cut to Taylor's face that would leave him permanently disfigured. As the outraged conductor continued to beat and kick Taylor, other passengers finally subdued the attacker. Taylor reported the event to Baldwin and to Washington. Baldwin, humiliated and outraged, suspended the conductor pending an investigation and apologized profusely to Washington.

Less than a year after the Atlanta Address the U.S. Supreme Court, in the landmark *Plessy v. Ferguson* case, declared that segregation in public transportation was not unconstitutional if equal accommodations were provided. The decision ushered in a half-century of segregation that permeated many other aspects of American life, including segregated housing, schools, and other public places such as restaurants. The highest court in the nation had declared segregation to be acceptable under the principal of separate but equal. It would take another half-century before the Supreme Court reversed the *Plessy* decision, admitting that separate was inherently unequal. While there is no direct connection between Washington's Atlanta speech and the Court's decision, since the *Plessy* case had originated four years earlier, both Washington's speech and the *Plessy* decision were harbingers of the times. Racial conditions in the South were growing worse, not better, even as Washington's personal fame and fortune were on the rise.

Washington did not invent racial segregation and disfranchisement; it was all around him at the time of the Atlanta Address. But it is equally true that his public acceptance of social inequality and his emphasis on gradual economic improvement instead of agitation for civil rights could not help but play into the hands of segregationists. Had he chosen protest and a demand for rights, which had been the hallmarks of earlier generations of abolitionists, he would have been cut to pieces by the powerful racist forces of his day. He would have been vilified and denounced as just one more "uppity darkey" who had forgotten his place in the racial pecking order of the South. Had Washington directly challenged the Jim Crow status quo, in other words, he would have lost. The question remains, by compromising and attempting to buy time for a racial settlement, did he not also fail? Washington's critics were yet to be heard from on this point. Their attack on Washington's program and his leadership would come later.

The fame that Washington gained from the Atlanta Exposition Address thrust him to the forefront as the leading black spokesman in America. The only person who had held this position before Washington was the great black abolitionist Frederick Douglass, who represented an earlier generation of race leadership in the long struggle to end slavery. Douglass has been born a slave in Maryland in 1817 but managed to escape to freedom when he was twenty years old. He became an eloquent spokesman for the abolition movement and a champion of women's rights and temperance. His fame spread with the publication of his autobiography in 1845.

Like Booker T. Washington, Douglass had a white father he did not know. Douglass learned to read when he was twelve, even though it was against the law, and later taught slaves to read the Bible until his school was destroyed by irate slaveowners wielding clubs. Like Washington too, Douglass knew the power that came with education and the ability to speak publicly. He trained himself as an orator by reading great speeches. Douglass's magnificent thunderous voice and his oratorical skills made him a powerful spokesman against the injustice of slavery. He later ran an abolitionist newspaper, the *North Star*, and was a favorite of the Republican party, having met with Abraham Lincoln and U. S. Grant.

By the time Booker T. Washington founded Tuskegee Institute in 1881, Douglass was sixty-three years old and had just published the third version of his autobiography. He was still an active speaker and public official, living in

Frederick Douglass, from an 1887 engraving. His death in 1895 left a void in race leadership.

Washington, D.C., where he held a number of Republican patronage posts including Recorder of Deeds for the District of Columbia and later minister to Haiti. His newspaper career was behind him, and he now spent much time at Cedar Hill, his beloved home overlooking the Anacostia River. Douglass was a lion in winter, but even in his old age he was a formidable figure with his great white mane of hair and his bushy white beard. The Sage of Anacostia could still arouse the passions of those who recalled his many years as a great champion of abolition.

Washington had some contact with Douglass, though the two men were not close friends. Washington had great respect for Douglass, but he also felt that the old fire-breathing speeches against slavery were a thing of the past. Slavery may have been defeated, but a racial settlement had not been achieved. In 1892 Washington had invited Douglass to be the commencement speaker at Tuskegee Institute. Tuskegee commencements were always important occasions that drew black farmers from the surrounding area to listen to the speeches and take part in the festivities. Douglass drew a large crowd, eager to see the most famous black man in America at the time. He was seventy-five, in poor health, and fewer than two years away from his death. He spoke on the topic of "Self-Made Men," and what he said that day complemented the Tuskegee philosophy. Douglass could still deliver an effective speech despite his advanced years and failing health. He declared the single most important thing that blacks needed to advance was education, and urged the graduating students to be thrifty and use common sense to get ahead. The Negro, he said, needed a "fair chance."

Douglass was impressed with what he saw at Tuskegee Institute. A reporter for the *Montgomery Advertiser* quoted him as saying "Verily, it would seem as if John's apocalyptic vision was realized and that he looked on a new heaven and a new earth."

It was perhaps no coincidence that when Booker T. Washington later delivered his Atlanta Address, he took the same popular passage from the twenty-first chapter of the Book of Revelation and predicted that the end of racial strife and the rise of justice for black Americans would bring to the South not only material prosperity but "a new heaven and a new earth."

Douglass died in February 1895, just seven months before Washington delivered the Atlanta Address. His death left a void in race leadership. Washington stepped into his shoes the very day he delivered his Atlanta speech. After more than a decade of developing his school and his program, Washington suddenly was an overnight success. In one of his most revealing statements about the impact of the Atlanta Address—where, for a moment at least, he threw away his usual caution and public humility—he wrote to the editors of the *New York World* that he thought his speech was the culmination of the work of abolitionists like William Lloyd Garrison and Frederick Douglass.

Years later he wrote with more customary modesty that until people began to write him letters urging him to assume the mantle of leadership left by Douglass, he did not have "the remotest idea that I should be selected or looked upon, in any such sense as Frederick Douglass had been, as a leader of the Negro people." But he continued to make a further distinction between himself and Douglass. While the old abolitionist had defended the race during slavery days, that long, bitter struggle did not equip him for the task of leading the race once slavery was ended. Washington said Douglass was not prepared to "to take up the equally difficult task of fitting the Negro for the opportunities and responsibilities of freedom." This task would require a different strategy; Washington's leadership would plan for the long haul. It would be gradual but cumulative in extending and expanding educational opportunities for blacks. It would mean making peace with former slavemasters. It would mean slow economic advancement that would ultimately lead to full citizenship and full acceptance by the dominant white culture. Blacks would succeed best if they pulled themselves up. In order for self-help programs to succeed, Washington needed time and cooperation from the white South.

Washington believed there were no quick fixes that would suddenly bring racial justice and equality to the millions of former slaves and their children. In his plan there was no place for hatred or looking backward, or for the fiery vengeance of the abolitionists. Frederick Douglass had challenged the slave system and the government that supported it. He had sought the destruction of the slave system through moral outrage. The leaders of the abolition movement refused to compromise with slavery and the slaveholding South. But how, Washington asked, could freedom be assured once slavery had ended? Could it happen if the old hatreds and the old fears remained, or if black leaders concentrated on civil rights and political agitation without first getting an education and a job? Washington's new kind of leader would be one who sought cooperation and friendship with the white South: "I felt," Washington wrote, "that we needed a policy, not of destruction, but of construction; not of defence, but of aggression; a policy, not of hostility or surrender, but of friendship and advance."

Historians have pondered just who made Washington the leading spokesman of his race. Why was it that he emerged as leader when others had similar ideas? Who appointed him? Was it influential whites from the North and South who saw in Washington a safe leader? Was it blacks who were looking for relief from the worsening racial climate in America? If he were promoted by the white establishment—the wealthy donors, the press, the politicians in the Republican party, the industrialists who looked at Southern blacks as a source of labor—wouldn't he then become a tool of these forces, a black leader beholden to whites? Washington's biographer Louis Harlan concluded that "it was white people who chose Washington to give the address, and white people's acclaim that established him as the Negro of the hour." Southern conservatives in charge of the Atlanta Exposition considered Washington a "safe" figure, Harlan wrote, and "blacks had virtually nothing to do with making Washington a black leader."

There is no question that Washington's conservative approach to race advancement made him acceptable to Southern white leaders. But Washington had to fight and negotiate with those same leaders of the exposition for the right to speak at its premier opening and not at the secondary ceremonies at the separate Negro Building. Too, Washington's reputation among blacks as an extraordinary educator preceded the Atlanta Address by many years. He had been called a Moses to his people even before the Atlanta speech. The best answer to the question of who made Washington the leader of his race is Washington himself. His steady rise to fame, his preparation, his drive, his personal story, his success at building Tuskegee Institute from nothing, his uncommon oratorical skills, his keen political instincts—these qualities and accomplishments made Washington the new leader. Whites easily accepted him, but so did blacks. There may have been some luck in it, but it was the kind of luck that comes from years of preparation for the arena. Washington was ready to lead, and he got the job largely on his own initiative. He was not a member of the Plucky Class at Hampton for nothing. He always saw himself going places, and he had a well-honed instinct not to let an opportunity pass by without grabbing it.

CHAPTER FIVE

The Modern Moses

And Moses lifted up his hand, and smote the rock with his rod twice; and water came forth abundantly, and the congregation drank. . . .—Numbers 20:11

The modern Moses, who leads his race and lifts it through Education to even better and higher things than a land overflowing with milk and honey.—Andrew Carnegie, speaking of Booker T. Washington, 1903

𝓙𝕖 Washington's instant fame did not alter his views on how to advance his race, nor did it change his dedication to his work at Tuskegee Institute. But it did open doors to him that had not been opened before. People now wanted to see and hear him. His speaking schedule continued to include small audiences in the North, where he went to raise money for Tuskegee, but he also joined the national lecture circuit, where his oratorical skills thrilled and delighted large white audiences. In the South he continued to speak to mostly black audiences. As before, he spoke often to the black residents of Macon County and the surrounding area.

Washington had a brief honeymoon with those who did not agree with the ideas in the Atlanta Address. Wherever blacks gathered to discuss matters related to race, the talk was of Washington and his speech. Francis J. Grimké, a leading black minister in Washington, D.C., whose white half-sisters were the well-known abolitionists Angelina and Sarah Grimké, reported to Washington that the Bethel Literary Society had discussed the Atlanta Address. "The opinions expressed by nearly all the speakers," he said, "were in commendation of the speech. There were a few who thought you were playing into the hands of the Southern Whites." Grimké himself would remain loyal to Washington for another decade before he too would condemn what he thought were the serious shortcomings of the Atlanta Address and of Washington's leadership.

The leading black clergyman Benjamin Tucker Tanner of Philadelphia wrote to Washington a week after the Atlanta Address, "I have read your magnificent oration at Atlanta with positive delight. Allow me to thank you for your noble utterances on behalf of the race; especially for the epigrammatic word: 'The opportunity to earn a dollar in a factory, is infinitely to be preferred in our present condition to the opportunity to spend a dollar in an opera.' God bless you for the word and make you more and more to increase in favor with God and man." Tanner would remain loyal to Washington's philosophy, but he later found reason to differ with Washington over the need to agitate for civil rights.

Regardless of his celebrity status, Washington would never leave the South. He would remain principal of Tuskegee Institute for the rest of his life. He would never hold political office. He would follow his own advice from the Atlanta Address and cast down his own bucket among the poorest of the poor in the Black Belt of Alabama. While he remained rooted in the region, he nonetheless spent a good part of his life traveling to the seats of power in the North—to New York, Boston, Chicago, and Washington, D.C.

Soon after the Atlanta Address, Washington used his newfound national voice to reiterate the cause of black education. One of the era's most flamboyant anti-black politicians, Benjamin Ryan Tillman of South Carolina, known as Pitchfork Ben, a former governor of the state and now a U.S. senator, had called for an end to support for black education in his state, suggesting that black schools should be funded by taxes raised by blacks themselves. It was not enough that the schools were segregated; school funding should be segregated too. Earlier, as governor, Tillman had set in motion the rewriting of South Carolina's constitution that disfranchised black voters in 1895.

At the urging of James Creelman of the *New York World*, Washington addressed an open letter to Tillman that was published in the *World*. This was an unusual tactic for Washington: writing to a white politician in another state and publishing the letter in a Northern newspaper. The letter was a blend of protest and obsequiousness. Washington fawned over Tillman with references to him as a member of the "great, intelligent Caucasian race," and calling him "Honored sir." Washington played the role of the humble black man born a slave: "I am no politician. I never made a political speech, and do not know as I ever shall make one, so it is not on a political subject that I address you."

He walked the tightrope expected of blacks when dealing with powerful whites. He was careful to couch his political views in a manner that would not offend Tillman or any white person in the South who read his letter. He wore the mask that blacks had learned to wear during nearly 250 years of slavery. He played out a time-tested role, demeaning on so many levels but also a form of diplomacy in a white world that considered the black race inferior. Washington played this game as well as anyone. He believed that humility, the ability to turn the other cheek, was not a sign of weakness or racial inferiority; it was how black people in the South conversed with whites in power. He had internalized this style early in his life. During slave times it had been honed and polished to the point where any slave knew how to "fool old massa." Whites like Tillman knew the game too. As race relations deteriorated over the years, Washington's critics would come to see his style as an embarrassment.

It was not lost on Tillman or anyone else who read the open letter that Washington was indeed injecting himself into politics, in this case the politics of education. Even so, Washington had to pretend that was not what he was talking about. While continuing to praise Tillman, he made his point that it would be absurd for South Carolina to turn its back on the education of 650,000 blacks in that state. He advanced the argument so that even a racist like Tillman would admire the logic of it. If South Carolina refused to support black education, Washington predicted that charitable organizations from across the country would step in to fill the gap. He wrote, "I believe, Senator Tillman, you are too great and magnanimous to permit this. I believe that the people of South Carolina prefer to have a large part in the education of their own citizens; prefer to have them educated to feel grateful to South Carolina for the larger part of their education rather than outside parties wholly."

Two years later Washington wrote another open letter to the Louisiana Constitutional Convention, which was debating the disfranchisement of blacks in that state as well as the need for property and educational qualifications for voting rights. Using the same careful tone he had employed in his earlier letter to Tillman, Washington reminded the Louisiana delegates that he was no politician but was writing merely as someone who had a "sincere love for our beautiful Southland." He urged the delegates not to disfranchise blacks. He agreed that some ballot restrictions might be needed to eliminate ignorance and corruption from government, but he expected such restrictions to be applied evenly to all regardless of race.

His open letter to the Louisiana convention appeared in several New Orleans papers and received positive editorial comment. Yet nothing Washington said halted the steady formalization of Jim Crow practices in the South. His conciliatory tone and acceptance of the way things were gave him the ability to speak out on virtually any subject as long as it was carefully phrased to avoid offending white sensibilities. He could protest injustice, but his protests were always qualified with such humility and caution that they lacked fire. Yet Washington always assumed he was being manly and forthright in his public utterances.

In September 1896 he wrote to the Christian Endeavor Society in a letter that was published in the society's magazine, *Golden Rule*. He urged its members to be brave and filled with Christian courage. "In many parts of our country," he wrote, "it requires much courage for a Christian to take a poor black boy by the hand and lead him to the Sunday school or Christian Endeavor Society." Thus he addressed the racial segregation of churches not by condemning the practice outright but by pointing out that it seemed to him to be unchristianlike behavior. "How often as a poor black boy have I passed the doors of churches and Sunday schools and heard the grand old song 'Come to Jesus,' welling up from hundreds of throats," he wrote, "and at the same time if I, a poor black boy, had obeyed the command, and entered that church or Sunday school, I should have been put out by force, if necessary."

With his race suffering under the yoke of growing racial oppression and disfranchisement, Washington nonetheless found his personal fortunes continuing to rise. In the same year of the Supreme Court's *Plessy* v. *Ferguson* decision, Harvard University conferred upon Washington an honorary master of arts degree, presenting him with another significant opportunity to extend his influence among prominent whites and the coming generation of America's elite. Thirteen distinguished Americans, including Washington, the only black man in the group, received honorary Harvard degrees in 1896, the most prominent being Nelson A. Miles, the Union general and recipient of the Medal of Honor, who had gained additional fame as an Indian fighter. On the evening of June 24, at the Harvard alumni dinner with everyone in their finest evening dress, Washington brought down the house with his opening line. As he looked out at the sea of white faces, he said, "I feel like a huckleberry in a bowl of milk." He was a man of substance, but he also realized he was interesting to many whites as an odd and interesting entertainment and an anomaly in this elite white setting.

In his talk at Harvard, Washington appealed to the wealthy and the well-bred to enlist in the cause of race uplift. "One of the most vital questions that touch our American life," he observed, "is how to bring the strong, wealthy, and learned into helpful touch with the poorest, most ignorant, and humble and at the same time, make the one appreciate the vitalizing, strengthening influence of the other. How shall we make the mansions on yon Beacon street feel and see the need of the spirits in the lowliest cabin in Alabama cotton fields or Louisiana sugar bottoms?" While his was only a brief after-dinner talk, Washington prophesized farther into the future than he did in most of his usual remarks. His gradualist approach to race advancement, and his willingness to endure wrongs in the name of eventual progress, seldom were stated more clearly than on that occasion.

> During the next half century and more, my race must continue passing through the severe American crucible. We are to be tested in our patience, our forbearance, our perseverance, our power to endure wrong, to withstand temptations, to economize, to acquire and use skill; our ability to compete, to succeed in commerce, to disregard the superficial

for the real, the appearance for the substance, and to be great and yet small, learned and yet simple, high and yet the servant of all. This, this is the passport to all that is best in the life of our republic, and the Negro must possess it, or be debarred.

Washington's public utterances on the best strategy for racial advancement in America would remain constant for the remainder of his life. He held tightly to concepts laid out in the Atlanta Address, seldom straying far from words he uttered on that fateful day in 1895, with the world watching him so closely. Washington delivered thousands of speeches in his lifetime, but they all sounded much like the Atlanta Address.

When once Washington tried to go beyond his Atlanta message, he found himself facing the wrath of Southern newspaper editors to such a degree that he retreated and apologized for what he had said. Such was the power of the Southern press to make Washington toe the line of his Atlanta speech. The occasion was the 1898 Peace Jubilee in Chicago celebrating the end of the Spanish-American War. The main national celebration was held in Chicago on October 16, in the magnificent, ornate Auditorium building, the pride of the city. This massive 4,300-seat theater with perfect acoustics, designed by Dankmar Adler and Louis Sullivan, was a splendid venue for a speaker like Booker T. Washington, whose conversational style and emotional appeals would echo throughout the hall. It was a great day for him personally: he appeared in the company of some of the nation's leading dignitaries, including President William McKinley and most of his cabinet.

Capitalizing on the patriotic fervor of the jubilee, Washington used the occasion to remind his listeners of the contributions and loyalty of black Americans in all the nation's wars. He applied the test of patriotism to blacks who had

Washington's speech at the Chicago Peace Jubilee in October 1898 was greeted by an overflowing, enthusiastic crowd. *(From The Story of My Life and Work)*

distinguished themselves in the American Revolution. He reminded his listeners that the first person killed at the Boston Massacre had been Crispus Attucks, a black man. His recitation moved on through the War of 1812, the Civil War, and the Spanish-American War. Each of Washington's patriotic points was met with such resounding cheers and applause that one newspaper described it as shaking the building to its very foundations. He repeated his speech at two other venues in Chicago, each to overflowing, enthusiastic crowds. Altogether on his visit Washington spoke to more than sixteen thousand persons. Newspapers in the North reported the event favorably, though only parts of his speech were printed.

It was not Washington's recitation of black patriotism that offended some Southern editors. It was his reference to racial prejudice in the South and his expression of hope that the successful conclusion of the Spanish-American War, with its black heroes, would be a good reason to bury prejudice and social separation. Clark Howell, editor of the *Atlanta Constitution*, attended the jubilee in Chicago. Howell had called Washington's Atlanta Address the "beginning of a moral revolution in America." But it was clear at the time, to Howell and many others, that Washington had defined the "moral revolution" to mean separate social lives for blacks. When the *Constitution* wrote about Washington's Peace Jubilee speech it noted Washington's reference to racial prejudice in the South and his departure from the Atlanta Address. Washington had said:

> But there remains one other victory for Americans to win—a victory as far-reaching and important as any that has occupied our army and navy. We have succeeded in every conflict, except the effort to conquer ourselves in the blotting out of racial prejudices. We can celebrate the era of peace in no more effectual way than by a firm resolve on the part of the Northern men and Southern men, black men and white men, that the trench which we together dug around Santiago, shall be the eternal burial place of all that separates us in our business and civil relations. Let us be as generous in peace as we have been in battle. Until we thus conquer ourselves, I make no empty statement when I say that we shall have, especially in the Southern part of our country, a cancer gnawing at the heart of the Republic, that shall one day prove as dangerous as an attack from an army without or within.

This would prove to be his boldest, most direct, and most prophetic utterance on race prejudice. Here Washington clearly went beyond a compromise with whites: he envisioned an end to separation between the races. His usual platitudes and rosy outlook gave way to a direct assault on racial prejudice. While he couched the problem in a national context, he added that racial prejudice was largely a problem of the South. There he was, in the North, in the presence of the President of the United States, attacking the South. It was most uncharacteristic, and several Southern newspapers quickly jumped on him.

The *Atlanta Constitution* seized on Washington's phrase calling for an end to separation in "business and civil relations," inferring that this included social relations. But not all Southern editors fell in line. E. W. Barrett, editor of the *Birmingham Age-Herald*, wrote to Washington, "You have doubtless seen many comments upon your Chicago speech. It is unnecessary for me to tell you in what newspapers they have appeared." Barrett offered Washington an opportunity to clear the air and give a full explanation of what he had said in Chicago in the pages of the *Age-Herald*. Two weeks after the Peace Jubilee speech, Washington's private secretary, the former Texas newspaperman Emmett J. Scott, cautioned Washington to avoid trying to explain himself and to take some time to gauge the extent of the criticism he had provoked. Scott thought it would be "unseemly to enter into a series of denials, etc., as this will be just what some people most desire that you should do, and it will tend to take from your manly plea and stand some of the strength which accentuated and impressed it." He reminded Washington, "*You* are now a great public character and cannot afford to engage every spiteful sensitive soul that attacks you." Scott said he stood ready to help Washington prepare an article of rebuttal should he decide to answer his critics.

Washington took part of Scott's advice: he refused to enter into a series of denials. Instead he sent a single letter to the editor of the *Birmingham Age-Herald*, published on November 10, 1898. In it Washington said he had always been consistent in articulating the proper course for the "elevation of the colored man." He had made it a rule not to say something before a Northern audience that he would not say in the South. He denied that his Peace Jubilee speech was any different, and specifically noted the phrase "business and civil relations" as similar to what he had said in Atlanta three years earlier. Then he added, "What is termed social recognition is a question I never discuss." He retreated to the formula of the Atlanta Address that condoned separate social lives for whites and blacks.

As to race prejudice, he told the *Age-Herald*, "In my address I very seldom refer to the question of prejudice because I realize that it is something to be lived down, not talked down." He refined his concept of race prejudice to broaden its meaning and make it more palatable to the South: "Whenever I discuss the question of race prejudice I never do so solely in the interest of the negro; I always take higher ground. If a black man hates a white man it narrows and degrades his soul. If a white man hates a black man it narrows and degrades his soul." These two sentences were carefully constructed by placing the black man as the agent of prejudice in the first sentence so that the logic of the second sentence, where the white man is culpable, could be seen as a reasonable conclusion.

Washington's letter to the *Age-Herald* had its intended effect: criticism of the Peace Jubilee speech faded. But Washington's concession, watering down what Emmett Scott called his "manly" statement in Chicago, was a costly compromise. Washington found safety in the formula of the Atlanta Address, the place where he had accepted racial segregation. He had many days of leadership ahead of him, but he would always be imprisoned by his retreat to the Atlanta Compromise. It would limit his leadership and ultimately lead to his downfall.

Taken together, the Atlanta Address in 1895, the Harvard Alumni dinner speech in 1896, and the Peace Jubilee Speech in 1898 all added to Washington's stature as a national celebrity. He was the only black man in the nation who could hobnob with captains of industry, major politicians, labor leaders like Samuel Gompers, and literary figures like Mark Twain. He knew he was famous and tried to make the most of his position to further the cause of race uplift and to ensure that his beloved Tuskegee Institute would survive and flourish. For the next few years his fame and his power continued to grow.

In an age when the very concept of "celebrity" held great fascination for a public eager for a good story, Washington thrived. Newspapers were the main means of communication that tied the nation together in a web of local and national news. It was the heyday of print, with thousands of independent newspapers serving small hamlets and big cities alike. Foreign-language papers reached the new immigrants in the cities, and a small but influential African-American press served blacks. During Washington's time there was a dramatic expansion of popular magazines eager to carry stories of the famous and how they lived. Washington's own autobiography was first serialized in *The Outlook*, a popular illustrated journal. Photography was just beginning to appear in newspapers and magazines, replacing line drawings made from zinc plates. In many local newspapers that were slow to adopt the new technology of halftone printing, Washington continued to appear in line drawings made earlier in life. His friendly, open, youthful face was familiar in many local newspapers long after he had begun to age, grow thicker in body, and exhibit more complex facial expressions.

Washington became the one black American whom everyone knew about and read about, whether they agreed with him or not. Reporters liked to follow him and cover his speeches. Editorial writers often used him as the best example of what an education and Christian values could do for members of his race. On the other hand, racist editorialists loved to jab at him and his program and look for weaknesses wherever they

This 1890 zinc engraving of a youthful Washington was used in many newspapers long after the widespread use of halftone photography was introduced in the early 1900s. *(Library of Congress)*

could be found. White people who perhaps knew no black person personally felt they knew Booker T. Washington. He became the role model for an entire race—and it was a heavy burden to bear. He met the challenge by always remaining publicly cheerful, positive, humble, and consistent. He never lost his temper in public, nor did he threaten or challenge his critics without control of his emotions. He expressed himself in measured tones. He was a master at wearing a mask that hid his doubts, fears, and disappointments. Even when fire-eating racists poked fun at him or portrayed him ruthlessly with demeaning racist slurs, Washington tried to stay above the fray—always turning the other cheek, always taking the high road, and always appearing to walk on the sunny side of the street even during the gloomiest days for him and his race.

Far more important than his newfound status as a national and international celebrity was the discovery of his real power. It came from millions of blacks who turned to him as their new Moses, but it also came from his acceptance in the highest circles of government, industry, and culture in America. For a man who never held political office, Washington would soon discover that he had more power to shape the racial issues facing the nation than any black person in American history to that time. His power would influence national politics, and he would build a complex network among blacks and whites who supported his programs and interests. Washington's critics referred to his growing network of influence as the Tuskegee Machine. It did operate like a political machine, with tentacles reaching far beyond Alabama into the boardrooms of top industrialists and eventually into the White House. The Tuskegee Machine also reached deep into the segregated world of black communities, where Washington's message was carried in black newspapers that were often subsidized by him, or whose editors were strong supporters of his philosophy and programs. But before the full scope of Washington's influence could be felt and before he could build his Tuskegee Machine and before he could expand his work for education in the South, he needed money.

Washington worked tirelessly to raise funds for Tuskegee's annual operating expenses. He lived out of a suitcase much of the year, staying in hotels in the North, where he went to raise money. If he were to realize his full potential as the leading spokesman of his race, and if he were to take his message and his program beyond the Black Belt of Alabama, he needed sums of money exceeding the immediate needs of Tuskegee Institute. It was only natural for him to approach some of the wealthiest men in America, especially those who had shown an interest in his work earlier and who would be willing to continue and even increase their financial aid to the new Moses.

Washington's reliance on the support of white philanthropists to build his school would now pay extra dividends with his newfound power. For more than a decade before the Atlanta Address he had built networks of white friends and supporters. Many of his earliest white followers were descendants of abolitionists and the Christian missionary movement that had moved into the South during Reconstruction to foster black education. Few of the missionary families that supported him could be said to have great wealth. Others, however, were rising industrialists like William Baldwin of the Southern Railroad and later the Long Island Railroad, who befriended Washington early on and became a Tuskegee trustee. Baldwin was the son of the founder of the Boston Young Men's Christian Union. He was in the vanguard of a new movement among some industrialists who believed that people who held economic power should be socially responsible. Baldwin was Washington's closest white friend and confidant for more than ten years before his early death from a brain tumor at the age of forty-two left Washington searching for someone to provide a new link to Northern industrialists who would support Tuskegee.

As time passed and Washington's fame grew he was able to tap America's wealthiest men, including John D. Rockefeller and H. H. Rogers of Standard Oil, and later John D. Rockefeller, Jr.; John Wanamaker, the wealthy New York department-store magnate and president of the Young Men's Christian Association; Julius Rosenwald, president of Sears, Roebuck and Company; Jacob Schiff, the Wall Street financier with extensive banking and railroad interests; and George Eastman, inventor of the Kodak camera. All these men, and others like them, aided Washington, Tuskegee Institute, and black education in the South in a variety of ways, some publicly and others privately, some with money and others with goods and services. Julius Rosenwald regularly sent railroad cars filled with Sears, Roebuck shoes—mostly factory seconds—that could be repaired in Tuskegee's shoe shop and distributed to students and to the poor in Macon County. More important, Rosenwald took an active part in recruiting other philanthropists and industrialists and arranged a number of railroad excursions to Tuskegee so that donors could see for themselves the kind of school Washington had built. In many ways Rosenwald was Baldwin's replacement: he joined the Tuskegee board of trustees and played an active role in the school's development and in Washington's career as a race leader.

H. H. Rogers of Standard Oil, often described as a tough and ruthless robber baron, liked to give money away privately and seemed delighted with the look on the faces of his recipients when he did. He once reached into his desk drawer, pulled out ten thousand-dollar bills, and handed them to Booker T. Washington for his work at Tuskegee. Washington was uncomfortable taking this much cash and insisted that Rogers at least make a record of his transactions and let a few people in on the gift so that Washington would be able to account for it. He and Rogers became friends. He toured Long Island Sound on Rogers's yacht and frequently visited him in New York City. Privately Rogers gave Washington smaller sums to support more than sixty other black schools in the South. George Eastman gave Tuskegee Institute at least $10,000 a year for more than a dozen years and donated another $250,000 when Washington died.

Many of these captains of industry and finance supported Washington for reasons of their own that had little to do with sentimentality, social responsibility, or altruism. While it would be unfair to suggest that their philanthropy toward black education or their support of Booker T. Washington was based solely on business considerations, these were hard-nosed businessmen, to be sure. They liked Washington's program of gradual but steady educational and economic growth, and his assumption that most black Americans were best suited to take jobs in agriculture, in the industrial sector as tradesmen, or as factory workers, both skilled and unskilled.

Industrialists like the men who supported Washington found themselves facing the rapid expansion and rising strength of trade unions. The first national railroad strike in 1877 had occurred just four years before Tuskegee Institute opened its doors. The owners and operators of America's industries saw in Washington a man who would not rock the boat. He was, after all, a conservative Republican during the heyday of the Republican ascendancy and the dominance of big business. Not an industrialist himself, he nevertheless thought like one. He was a safe and sane leader who would not encourage strikes and unions. Just as Washington eschewed politics and agitation as tactics to advance the race, he would not agitate for workers' rights much beyond saying that a man deserved a fair wage for a fair day's work. He was not a union man. Washington opposed unions primarily because he saw them as impediments to black labor. Trade unions in particular were for whites only. Washington was less concerned about the potential for exploitation of black workers than about the possibility they might be cut out entirely from industrial jobs that were being filled by millions of immigrants.

Looking back on Washington's view of labor more than twenty years after his death, James Weldon Johnson, writer, poet, and longtime leader of the NAACP, noted that Washington's understanding of the labor situation in America was at the heart of his genius as a leader. Washington recognized that traditional black jobs were being lost to immigrants and to changing cultures. Johnson described a secure black "industrial zone" in the South that had been protected by Southern mores going back into slave times. Some jobs white men simply would not take during slavery or afterward. These jobs, meager though they might seem today, were incredibly important to poor people who had little else available to them. Traditionally black jobs included barbers, laundresses, and waiters. Black women working as laundresses could hold families together, but newfangled steam laundries were putting them out of business. By 1938, when Johnson wrote his observations, white girls had all but replaced black men as waiters. In an example of "doubly inverted Jim Crow," white men in the South, who had always preferred black barbers, found white men holding razors to their throats.

Washington may not have seen eye to eye with the motives of some American industrialists, but his outlook was similar enough that mutual benefits were possible. The industrialists wanted a steady and reliable labor pool that would not agitate against them; Washington needed the industrialists for the money and jobs they could provide for his people. When William Baldwin managed the Southern Railway, he employed thousands of blacks, mostly for manual labor. This fact was not lost on Booker T. Washington.

Later generations of Washington's critics would look harshly on his reliance on wealthy whites to advance his school and his race leadership. But where does one go for money if he does not have his own? There were no black industrialists. Washington befriended wealthy white patrons to help him do his work. He fit right in with what Mark Twain called the Gilded Age, a time of unbridled capitalism and the worship of the almighty dollar. Washington thought like a capitalist even if he had no money or an industry of his own. He genuinely liked being with the rich and famous and the movers and shakers of society. What he really wanted was a share of their material success that could be spread to black America. He envisioned that day when blacks would be captains of industry, if only his race could get a leg up and into the system of American capitalism that had produced so much wealth. The nation was awash in money, but little of it was finding its way into the growing ghettos of black life.

Booker T. Washington's rise to fame also coincided with the rising popularity of Social Darwinism, the theory that sought to explain why some people and some races excelled while others failed in life's competition. Social Darwinism took its name from and was based loosely on Charles Darwin's recently advanced theory of evolution. It was the brainchild of the British philosopher Herbert Spencer and was championed in the United States by Yale professor William Graham Sumner, who attempted to apply the theory of biological evolution to human cultural and economic evolution. Just as species evolve by a natural selection of traits necessary for survival, Sumner suggested, the same could be applied to the human competition for survival in society. Those who survive most successfully—the wealthy and the powerful—would show the clearest signs of social fitness and thus would be superior to those who lacked the competitive qualities needed for social and economic success.

Social Darwinism, as expressed by Sumner, could be applied to Washington's program of race uplift through thrift, industry, hard work, and education. Human competition, according to Sumner, was best expressed in terms of the "acquisition of material goods by industry, energy, skill, frugality, prudence, temperance, and other industrial virtues." After slavery, many blacks defined freedom as being able to work for oneself and not be compelled by another man. But what did freedom mean twenty-five years later in an age of unregulated, free-market American capitalism? Freedom, to the Social Darwinists, was tied to owning property and doing with it as desired, without interference from other people or from government. Social Darwinism accepted the notion that inequality was a fact of life. Only the fittest would acquire property and the success that went with it.

While Social Darwinism filled the air, it had its critics too. Henry George, who would later become famous for his Single Tax program, agreed with the Social Darwinists on the importance of owning property but disagreed that land would ever be redistributed for social good under the laissez-faire assumptions of the free market. Active intervention would be necessary to spread wealth more equitably in America.

George wrote in 1879 that the central problem in America was the vast gulf between the rich and poor. Washington saw this gulf every day in the lives of poor black people in Alabama who did not yet have the freedom to control their own labor. They were landless; they had to work for those who owned the land. Landowners ultimately controlled their labor. George concluded that "Equality of political rights will not compensate for the denial of the equal right to the bounty of nature." The bounty of nature was the land itself and the wealth that land produced in crops and minerals. This powerful idea—that political rights meant nothing if you did not own property, especially land, from whence all wealth flowed—was also at the heart of Washington's belief that an economic foundation must precede political rights. Like George, he understood that political rights were secondary to the power that comes from the acquisition of land and wealth. Without these, the wealthy would always control the exercise of political rights as well as being the providers of jobs.

In the ideas put forth by Social Darwinists, a man like Andrew Carnegie, the wealthiest man in America, who had beaten all the competition and moved up the social and economic scale, would represent the pinnacle of social evolution. Social Darwinism went hand in hand with the Gilded Age notion that the ultimate goal of any red-blooded American was to become rich and influential. Acquiring wealth was no accident, according to Social Darwinism; it was ethnically and racially inspired.

The negative implications of Social Darwinism were profound: those who were poor must be inferior on the evolutionary scale. Taken too literally, Social Darwinism was nothing but racism covered with a thin academic veneer. It condemned whole peoples and races, including black Americans. Andrew Carnegie himself thought some of the conclusions of the Social Darwinists were extreme but did not disagree with the general concept. In his book *Triumphant Democracy*, he wrote that America was composed of highly successful people, mostly of British stock, who had proven their superiority. But rather than stop with this unchecked view of racial and ethnic superiority, Carnegie went on to say that the rich should help the less fortunate and the inferior races, as he saw them, through philanthropy. He modified Social Darwinism to include the notion that the fittest in society had an obligation to the less fortunate so they too might become better at the game of socioeconomic competition.

There is little evidence that Washington was a particular student of Social Darwinism, but its language and ideas were all around him as he developed his own ideas about race advancement. He did, however, study a modified version of Social Darwinism that interested him, and that he was able to exploit successfully for his own ends.

No one fascinated Washington more than Andrew Carnegie, and eventually no one would help him more than

Carnegie. Carnegie's story of advancement from humble origins deeply appealed to Washington. So did Carnegie's money. In 1889 Carnegie wrote an extended essay called *The Gospel of Wealth* that was especially appealing to Washington. Carnegie claimed it was the responsibility of those who had amassed great fortunes to give their money away to improve society. Wealthy people should act as trustees of their wealth and use prudent judgment in making it available for purposes that advanced humanity. Carnegie loathed the idea that great fortunes would be frittered away by those—including family—who had nothing to do with creating the wealth in the first place. He sold his vast steel holdings and began giving his millions away to build libraries and endow worthy enterprises.

W. E. B. Du Bois told this story of his chance encounter with Booker T. Washington on an elevated train in New York City. Washington, headed for an appointment with Andrew Carnegie, asked Du Bois if he had ever read Carnegie's *Gospel of Wealth*. Du Bois said he had not. Washington told him he should, because Carnegie "sets great store by it." Du Bois interpreted this to mean that Washington was a cynic and a panderer who would say and do anything to please white people if they gave him money. Yet there is much evidence to suggest just the opposite was true. Washington liked the idea of *The Gospel of Wealth*; he believed it. He saw it as a potential lifeline for his race. If more wealthy whites would engage in philanthropy on the scale of Carnegie, it would hasten the day when blacks would have better schools, better jobs, and better prospects for success. Du Bois may have been correct to see pandering in Washington's approach to Carnegie, but he overlooked the fact that Washington too "set great store by" *The Gospel of Wealth* and its author.

Andrew Carnegie, a Scottish immigrant, had entered the United States with his family in 1848 when he was thir-

The richest man in America, Andrew Carnegie was Booker T. Washington's chief benefactor. *(Library of Congress)*

teen years old. With hardly a cent to his name, he worked as a child laborer, saving his pennies and always trying to improve his station in life. Through luck, hard work, and smart investments, he became the wealthiest man in America, sitting atop a colossal steel empire at the time Washington delivered the Atlanta Address. Carnegie's story of rags to riches was not an Horatio Alger fable, it was the real thing. America was filled with stories like this, but few, if any, matched Carnegie's. Some of his money would trickle down to Booker T. Washington. For a man of great wealth like Carnegie, it wasn't a magnificent sum, but it was a godsend to Washington. It freed him from financial worries and gave him sufficient resources to extend his personal power as well as his leadership network.

With the publication of Washington's autobiography *Up from Slavery* in 1901, his considerable fame increased many times over. He was nearing the peak of his influence as the new century dawned. He had written the first major black version of the rags-to-riches success story. The book was well received in a nation that thrived on such stories to reinforce common beliefs about the American dream, even for a humble slave child like Booker Washington. When Carnegie read the book he was so taken by it that he immediately wished to help Washington and his work. In 1903 an agreement was reached with Washington's friend William Baldwin acting as the middleman. Carnegie gave Tuskegee Institute $600,000 in 5 percent U.S. Steel bonds—a considerable fortune at the time.

The gift was announced publicly, but some of its provisions were kept private. Carnegie wanted $150,000 of the bonds set aside for Washington and his family, to make sure he could continue his work as a race leader without having to worry about his own salary. Washington was concerned that he would be compromised in the South if people thought he was now wealthy. He also figured that such a sum coming to him personally would hurt his future fundraising efforts. His keen sense of how this large gift would be seen, especially in the South, led him to ask Carnegie to modify the gift. In a private meeting in the steel magnate's mansion, the personal money was turned over to the Tuskegee trustees. Washington argued that he and his wife did not have elaborate personal needs, and he was sure the trustees would act properly to take care of them. Washington thus gave up his Tuskegee salary and relied on the trustees to fund his speaking tours and take care of his personal finances, which they did.

Carnegie explained his gift by saying that he considered Washington one of the foremost men of his time, with a unique mission to uplift a race. He called Washington a "modern Moses":

A political cartoon from the *Boston Record*, April 25, 1903, shows Washington's ability to get money from Andrew Carnegie. It is based on the biblical story of Moses striking rocks with his rod to produce water.

History is to know two Washingtons, one white, the other black, both Fathers of their People. I am satisfied that the serious race question of the South is to be solved wisely, only by following Booker T. Washington's policy which he seems to have been specially born—a slave among slaves—to establish, and even in his own day, greatly to advance.

When Washington returned to Tuskegee after negotiating the Carnegie gift, the entire school turned out to greet him. Flags waved, the crowd cheered, students lifted large portraits of Carnegie and Washington, and the band played "See the Conquering Hero Comes." It was the beginning of

Three of Washington's white allies, photographed in 1906—from left, John Wanamaker, William H. Taft (then secretary of war), Washington, and Andrew Carnegie. *(Library of Congress)*

a long and fruitful relationship between Washington and the wealthiest man in America. Not only would Tuskegee benefit, but with Washington's continuing appeals to Carnegie, many other leading black schools in the South would receive his philanthropy. Carnegie, living out the ideas set forth in his *Gospel of Wealth*, proceeded to give his millions away partly by building libraries on campuses and in towns and cities across the nation. One political cartoon at the time of Carnegie's bounteous gift to Tuskegee, published in the *Boston Record* and other newspapers, shows Booker T. Washington, dressed in flowing robes, tapping his staff on a big rock with Andrew Carnegie's face on it while gold coins flow out of the rock. The caption reads: "The 'Modern Moses' Strikes Rocks!"

Through Carnegie, Washington had found a good part of the money he needed to help him promote black education in the South. It could also be used to expand his behind-the-scenes political influence and build his extensive network of power that became known as the Tuskegee Machine. For the remaining years of his life, no one in black America would equal him in power and influence. Much of what he did would remain hidden, because he could not survive in Jim Crow America if the South knew the full extent of his ability to cross the color line and act an adviser to captains of industry and even to presidents of the United States.

CHAPTER SIX

Inside the Briar Patch

*. . . But do please, Brer Fox, don't fling me in dat brier-patch.
. . ."*—Joel Chandler Harris, *Uncle Remus: His Songs and Sayings,* 1881

Blessed are the meek: for they shall inherit the earth.—Matthew 5:5

𝕁𝕊 In the same year that Booker T. Washington founded Tuskegee Institute, the Southern writer Joel Chandler Harris published the first of his popular Uncle Remus books based on folktales told by slaves. These tales, some with African origins and others derived from classical antiquity such as Aesop's fables, featured animals whose situations paralleled human situations. The hero of the tales was often a rabbit who managed to outwit his cunning and more powerful adversary, the fox. Sometimes the fox had to outwit his adversaries. Harris's stories, written in a Negro dialect, were, in many ways, a literature perfectly representative of Jim Crow America. If a black person was to outwit his white adversary during slave days or during its Jim Crow aftermath, he or she often had to do it with cunning, deception, and secrecy.

In the original edition of Webster's blue-back speller, the most influential book in Washington's childhood, was another tale derived from Aesop, entitled "The Fox in the Brambles." In this tale a fox had to hide in a thorny bramble bush to avoid capture by vicious dogs. The thorns pricked the fox and made him bleed. But he had enough sense to stay in the brambles because he knew his life depended on it. He had to suffer so he could survive. Even though the brambles hurt him, they gave him protection.

It would be hard to imagine more suitable tales to justify Washington's strategy of accommodation to white power than Aesop's Fox in the Brambles or Uncle Remus's Bre'r Rabbit. To survive in a world where powerful forces aligned to keep blacks under control in a second-class status in America took carefully honed survival skills and a lot of suffering. It meant dealing with the frustration and pain of waiting in the briar patch for the time when those in pursuit would go away.

Washington learned how to fight Jim Crow and outwit his enemies. He did it from inside the protection of Tuskegee Institute, from inside the thorny thicket of American racism that imprisoned blacks during the Jim Crow era. While he always showed his public face of humility, optimism, and hope, he worked behind the scenes in great secrecy to challenge racial injustice, to fight segregation in public transportation, and to find ways to change the system that held his race in check. In secrecy he would hire lawyers to challenge Jim Crow laws, employ spies to watch his white adversaries and his black critics, use code words in secret correspondence, and take advantage of his personal influence with prominent whites in positions of power.

Washington's underground personality was more militant and complex than his public face. Many of his secret actions remained hidden even from his close associates, and he often suffered public criticism from blacks for his lack of action even when he was actually working behind the scenes. Did Washington's secret life, his private fight against Jim Crow, amount to much? Did private actions offset his accommodating public persona? Such questions unearth a still greater issue: Is it possible to make social and political progress without open conflict?

Washington was up against large historical forces not of his making and beyond his control. The Reconstruction Era federal government had failed to live up to its promise of political equality for blacks. When Reconstruction ended, so-called White Redeemers recaptured control of politics in Southern states and restored the land to its previous owners. In doing so the South regained control of the black population, where the masses of newly freed slaves found themselves working as sharecroppers under the watchful eye, in many instances, of their former masters. This successful Southern counterrevolution undid for blacks the promise of the Thirteenth, Fourteenth, and Fifteenth Amendments.

Nowhere in Washington's voluminous correspondence did he ever express the need to fight Jim Crow openly. Is a revolution possible without an open fight and without casualties? It took 600,000 casualties in the Civil War to end slavery. What would it take to end Jim Crow? This was Washington's dilemma. His attempt at appeasement, his accommodation to white rule, was designed to give black America time to overcome the legacy of slavery and the failure of Reconstruction. Washington did not think his people were strong enough to survive a direct confrontation. Seeing no way to win in open conflict with white America, he planned a gradual approach to advancement. It would be a painful waiting period, a time when he and his race would hunker down in the briar patch and attempt to survive, hoping for a better day. He was trying to buy time for the race to progress and get on its feet after centuries in bondage and its virtual reenslavement following Reconstruction.

In the North Washington operated differently from his practices in the South. When in the South he seldom violated the code of conduct established for blacks. He did not mix socially with whites in the South, even though he did this regularly in the North. Sometimes his Northern activities got him into trouble, as they did in 1898 when he escorted the white daughter of one of Tuskegee's donors, John Wanamaker, into a Saratoga Springs hotel for dinner. The Southern press chastised Washington on this occasion for not following his own message, that blacks and whites could be as separate as the fingers in all things social. Fortunately Washington moved about freely in Northern cities like Boston, New York, or Chicago. He slept in the best white hotels, dined in fine restaurants, and easily crossed the color line, which was not so sharply drawn in the North, especially in the cities, as it was in the South.

Washington always insisted that Tuskegee students be on their best behavior when they were in the town of Tuskegee. They were to stay out of trouble, lest it reflect poorly on the school. He constantly reminded students of their duty to protect the school's reputation. The campus was their refuge. Its black faculty and student body represented an accepted and approved enclave, segregated by choice and by circumstance. The faculty, too, was to avoid any racially related controversy that might jeopardize the institution. A faculty member exhibiting drunkenness, insolence, or defiance was shown the door. Tuskegee Institute could not risk such behavior. It was Washington's first love, the source of his fame, the model for inspiring blacks to obtain an education, and an even greater model of black self-help. He could point to Tuskegee as a showcase of black progress, which he did at every opportunity.

But Tuskegee was also his base of operations—the fulcrum of his political leverage and a safe harbor for the growth of his far-flung empire of influence. Washington assembled a staff at Tuskegee and elsewhere that worked on his behalf

The executive council of Tuskegee Institute, photographed by Frances Benjamin Johnston in 1902. From left, top row, Robert R. Taylor, R. M. Attwell, Julius Ramsey, Edgar J. Penney, Matthew T. Driver, Henry G. Maberry, George Washington Carver. Bottom row, Jane E. Clark, Emmett J. Scott, Booker T. Washington, Warren Logan, John H. Washington (Booker T. Washington's brother). Not shown: Roscoe C. Bruce, Charles H. Gibson, Margaret M. Washington. *(Library of Congress)*

writing speeches, handling publicity, monitoring race news from across the country, and freeing him from a great deal of administrative routine. Foremost among his loyal lieutenants was Emmett Scott, his private secretary, who carefully managed and nurtured Washington's growing network with skill and talent. It is hard to imagine Washington without Scott at his side. Their correspondence is extensive, candid, and always businesslike and professional. While they used the telephone when separated, they preferred the less expensive forms of communication, letters and telegrams. Because Scott meticulously saved Washington's correspondence, it remains a valuable resource that reveals how they worked together.

When Washington was away from Tuskegee, as he often was, Scott and a few other officers at the school, such as the school treasurer, Warren Logan, were in charge of daily operations. In Washington's absence, Scott not only kept an eye on happenings at Tuskegee and reported immediately on any potential trouble, he also monitored major newspapers, both black and white, to keep Washington abreast of any story or event that would bear on matters of race. Through a clipping service, Scott arranged to gather regularly all newspaper stories about Washington and Tuskegee. Washington's third wife, Margaret, also served as his eyes and ears on campus when he was away.

With a few notable exceptions, such as the Wanamaker dinner, Washington could move about freely in the North. His fund-raising trips were legitimate reasons for him to be in the company of Northern whites and seldom raised eyebrows in the Southern press. He often took the Tuskegee Choir with him to entertain possible donors with Southern melodies and old slave songs. But during these many trips to the North he also met with allies, conducted the business of the race, planned strategies, and crossed the color line with relative impunity. In his public statements he always denied that he was a politician, but behind the scenes he ran a sophisticated political operation that reached into black communities across the country and kept him in touch with wealthy industrialists and prominent Republican politicians.

One hot summer night in June 1895, an incident occurred that illustrated how Washington had to act secretly to protect his school while helping a man who was being chased by a lynch mob for crossing the color line. The incident also brought into sharp relief the shortcomings of Washington's

Emmett Jay Scott was Washington's private secretary and the chief executive of his empire of power and influence. Photograph by Frances Benjamin Johnston, 1902. *(Library of Congress)*

philosophy that the best way for blacks to advance was to get an education and a job.

The Jim Crow system accepted black farmers, mechanics, and even teachers, but other occupations, especially the law profession, raised suspicions among whites. In the town of Tuskegee lived a black lawyer named Thomas A. Harris. He had been born into slavery and had served as a body servant for a Confederate officer during the Civil War. Active in black Republican politics during Reconstruction, Harris had been a student for a year at Tuskegee Institute in the early days of the school's existence more than a decade earlier, from 1883 to 1884. By the nature of his occupation Tom Harris was already pushing the boundaries of the color line. He was not well liked among the white population, and even Washington had his doubts about the man. The *Tuskegee News* described Harris as being "unpopular with his own race on account of his airs of superiority." Washington saw him a potential source of trouble all too close to home. His suspicions were eventually confirmed.

Harris had invited a white preacher to dinner at his home. Later the preacher was seen walking on the streets of Tuskegee between Harris's two attractive young daughters, holding an umbrella for them. Such a blatant display of social mixing of the races led a white mob to run the preacher out of town. The "yankee preacher," as the *Tuskegee News* called him, was also alleged to have been talking up social equality. Members of the mob were not satisfied: here was just one more good reason for them to get rid of Tom Harris too. They sent Harris a letter ordering him to get out of town by six o'clock in the evening on June 8 or there would be trouble.

By the time Harris received the letter it was already past the deadline. The letter had been picked up at the post office late that day by his son Wiley, a local butcher. Since Wiley had no reason to know the letter's contents, he did not deliver it immediately. Soon the normally quiet night streets of Tuskegee were alive with the sounds of barking dogs and a mob on the move. A group of masked men was headed for Harris's house, torches blazing. It was as if the Ku Klux Klan had been reborn in the sleepy town of Tuskegee. Harris, in a panic, got into a scuffle with one of his white neighbors who tried to hold him for the mob. When the mob approached, one man pulled a gun and fired at Harris at close range, expecting to kill him; but the bullet missed Harris and struck the white neighbor in the neck. Harris ran as more shots rang out. He was shot in the leg, shattering the bone, and fell in the street bleeding and screaming for help. In the melee, attention shifted to the wounded white man, giving Harris's family a chance to carry him off the street.

Later that night Wiley Harris carried his wounded father in a wagon to the front door of Booker T. Washington's home on the campus of Tuskegee Institute. By the time the lynch mob arrived searching for him, Harris and his son had disappeared. The angry, armed men demanded that Washington turn Harris over to them. Washington sought to calm them. He said that Harris had come to him for help, but when he learned that Harris was in trouble with town citizens he sent Harris away and told him he could not take refuge at the school. Washington told just enough of the truth to quiet the passions of the mob. He had not lied about Harris being on the campus, nor about him being sent away. The mob left believing that Washington did the right thing. An account in the *Tuskegee News* a few days after the incident praised Washington for conducting himself "in the most prudent and conservative manner" when he refused to help Harris.

What really happened that night was discovered during research many years later. In the wake of the Harris incident, a number of prominent blacks were troubled by reports that Washington would not help a man in need and had turned him away. After the Atlanta Address later that year, some blacks wondered if they could trust a man like Washington to lead them when he would do a thing like this. Finally the black minister Francis Grimké wrote to Washington and asked for an explanation.

Washington told Grimké that "I could not take the wounded man into the school and endanger the lives of students entrusted by their parents to my care to the fury of some drunken white men." Instead he had arranged to hide Harris off campus and then get him to Montgomery for medical treatment, which Washington paid for out of his own pocket. In effect, Washington hid Harris in the briar patch, using time-honored methods honed during slavery of saving a black life while fooling a white mob. Harris would later write to thank Washington for his help. He had recovered from his wound, but one leg was shorter than the other, he said. Seven years later, after moving about in other Alabama towns, Harris returned to Tuskegee and lived there for a while in 1902 before moving on again.

In his explanation to Grimké, Washington wrote, "I simply chose to help and relieve this man in my own way rather than in the way some man a thousand miles away would have had me do it." He would use this phrase in a number of his speeches over the years to remind blacks, especially those in the North, that criticism of his actions from afar was easy, but that living and working in the South had its special challenges.

Washington's extensive "secret life" was at the heart of his role as a leader in the South. His actions were shaped by the Jim Crow world in which he lived, not, as he said, by someone living a thousand miles away. His elaborate network of contacts with individuals and organizations and especially with the black press made his secret life possible. This network, the so-called Tuskegee Machine, made all else possible. Tuskegee Institute was the perfect, segregated, self-contained briar patch from which to work, plan, and scheme on behalf of his race. It offered Washington the public mantle of a prominent educator while hiding his aggressive and sometimes ruthless actions as a political boss who operated on both sides of the color line. The key ingredient to his actions behind the scenes often was the use of friends and paid agents to do the work without a direct connection that was traceable to Washington.

Through his friendship with T. Thomas Fortune, for example, Washington was able to take an existing organization, the National Afro-American Council, and direct it for his own purposes. Fortune, a black journalist and one of the most brilliant, incisive, and passionate observers of the worsening aspects of Jim Crow America, traveled extensively in the South. His book *Black and White in America*, published in 1884, decried the virtual reenslavement of blacks as sharecroppers. Fortune had grown up in a part of Florida where the Ku Klux Klan was strong. His own father, a tanner and shoemaker, was hounded by the Klan for his political activities and for mingling with white people. Fortune's passion for his cause made his newspaper, the *New York Age*, the best black paper in the country.

Fortune was also the driving force behind the National Afro-American League, founded in 1887 as the first national civil rights organization to focus on black conditions in the South. It had a short life. Failing to attract much black support, it lacked funds to challenge Jim Crow laws in court, and by 1893 it was defunct. When Fortune's travels through the South brought him to Tuskegee in the 1890s, he became a convert to Washington's philosophy. The two men became friends and allies, and Fortune became a prominent partner in Washington's rise to power. In many ways Fortune helped create Washington's public persona as the copy editor of Washington's first autobiography, *The Story of My Life and Work* (1900), and later as ghostwriter for other of Washington's publications and speeches. Fortune came to represent one of the central cogs of the Tuskegee Machine. His influential newspaper became an organ for Washington's program, and Washington's money heavily subsidized the *New York Age*. After the Afro-American League disbanded in 1893, Washington helped Fortune to revive the League in 1898 under a new name, the National Afro-American Council.

T. Thomas Fortune, the leading black journalist of the Jim Crow era, was a close friend of Washington and an important player in promoting his program even though he was more militant.

The council's first meeting in the fall of 1898 was literally a thousand miles from Tuskegee, Alabama, in Rochester, New York. It brought together existing black organizations across a spectrum of benevolent, religious, and political groups. Bishop Alexander Walters of the A.M.E. Zion church and Fortune were the most prominent leaders, though early members included W. E. B. Du Bois and the black writer Ida B. Wells-Barnett. The council contributed to a number of court cases fighting disfranchisement in Louisiana and one case in Alabama, *Giles v. Harris*, that in 1903 reached the Supreme Court.

From the very start Washington saw the National Afro-American Council as a tool for his own work. He used Fortune to further his agenda, but it was a two-way street.

Fortune benefitted from subsidies to his paper, and Washington eventually became a silent part-owner of the *New York Age*. Fortune also relied on Washington as someone to help him with his persistent alcohol problem. Their friendship was deep and personal, but Washington always kept a watchful eye on Fortune for fear he would take to the bottle and say or write something that would jeopardize their collaboration. Fortune was more militant than Washington, and in private he could be sharply critical of his benefactor, something Washington tolerated from Fortune more than he did from others.

With Fortune's support, in fewer than four years all the officers and most of the members of the Afro-American Council were Washington's loyal supporters. The council became little more than a front for Washington's program of accommodation and his cautious approach to any direct challenges to Jim Crow. Both Du Bois and Ida B. Wells-Barnett resigned from the council as more and more "Booker-ites" came to dominate the organization. By 1908 the council ceased to exist. Many of those who were vocal critics of Washington had by then resigned from the council. Some of them would reemerge in the Niagara Movement and later with the NAACP.

Washington also sought to control the black press in the United States. He succeeded to a great extent since many black newspapers were run with little capital, and Washington's subsidies—both directly as cash and indirectly as advertising revenue—helped them make ends meet. It was easier and safer for black editors in the South to support Washington, but his influence extended into the black communities of Northern cities as well. Scarcely a black newspaper in the United States was not influenced in some manner by him. Likewise, as magazines grew in importance in the early twentieth century, Washington realized their influ-

ence on people's attitudes, politics, and social life. A half-
dozen black magazines emerged in the first decade of the
new century. One of the most ambitious, *The Voice of the
Negro*, was founded by a white publisher, Austin Jenkins,
whose firm, J. L. Nichols & Company, had published Washington's first autobiography. Washington told the publisher
that he supported the effort because his race needed a first-
class magazine. Emmett Scott served on the *Voice*'s editorial
board. Privately Washington wrote to Scott suggesting that
he have a heart-to-heart talk with the publisher to make
sure the magazine toed the Washington line.

The Voice of the Negro was supposed to be a broad-based
magazine, impartial to the growing feud between Washington and his critics. An editorial in the first issue promised
to be a "sensible, practical magazine for all the people." But
its editor, J. Max Barber, also promised, in the muckraking
style of the day, to expose and shock people with revela-
tions. When the first issue appeared in 1904 it prominently
featured an article by Washington that had been edited by
Scott. Subsequent issues, however, displeased Washington,
who sensed in Barber a troublemaker. Washington visited
the offices of the magazine in Chicago to complain of Barber's news columns to the president of the publishing firm,
John A. Hertel. Without telling Barber the source of the
criticism, Hertel conveyed Washington's concerns. Barber
knew instantly what had happened and wrote to Emmett
Scott that he was under pressure to knuckle under to the
Tuskegee line, which he resented. The next few issues of the
magazine included articles by Mrs. Booker T. Washington,
and prominently placed advertisements for Tuskegee.

Through Scott, in 1904 Barber asked Washington to write
a letter of introduction for him so that he could interview
Theodore Roosevelt's campaign manager, George Cortelyou.
Washington refused, sensing that Barber might interfere

with Washington's close ties to Roosevelt. This was the last straw for Barber, who then wrote a snide attack on Washington in the December 1904 issue of *The Voice of the Negro*. In "What Is a Good Negro?" and without mentioning Washington by name, Barber wrote: "A good Negro is one who says that his race does not need the higher learning: that what they need is industrial education, pure and simple." In the January 1905 issue Barber included an item by W. E. B. Du Bois charging that "hush money" in the amount of $3,000 was being used to subsidize black newspapers in five cities. Washington's name was not mentioned, but there was no doubt about the reference.

Scott then resigned from the magazine's editorial board. Writing to Hertel and Jenkins, he said he could no longer tolerate Barber's "overweening egoism." Jenkins responded that he was glad Scott was resigning, that this cleared the air about any conflict the magazine had regarding Washington's influence. In the same letter Jenkins reported that he had word that Washington was part-owner of another black magazine, the *Colored American Magazine*, published by Jenkins's rival, Doubleday and Page. Both Scott and Washington denied Washington's secret part-ownership of the new magazine, though it was true.

Washington's double-dealing and attempts to control *The Voice of the Negro* continued unabated. Hertel and Jenkins formed a new company that published Washington's next book, ghostwritten by T. Thomas Fortune, *The Negro in Business*. Washington complained to Jenkins that he could not understand how the company could publish and promote his book and then undermine his work in the pages of the magazine. But he continued to deny involvement with the *Colored American Magazine*. In this instance, and others like it, Washington, aided and abetted by Scott, simply could not resist attempting to control the newspapers and magazines that affected his work and his carefully constructed public image. He never let up, continuing his assault on *The Voice of the Negro* and J. Max Barber until the magazine was driven out of business in 1907. Black newspapers under Washington's control attacked *The Voice of the Negro* at every opportunity and found reason to belittle the editor when the offices of the magazine were moved to a segregated section in Atlanta. Stories about this move featured the image of Barber's white publishers opening his mail and then sending it to the building where the black editor worked, a building in which he had to take the freight elevator to get to his office. During the Atlanta Riot of 1906 Barber claimed that some of the stories of blacks raping white women were actually done by whites in black face. He had to flee Atlanta until things calmed down. Meanwhile Booker T. Washington and W. E. B. Du Bois rushed to Atlanta to offer help to the victims. Washington and Scott saw to it that Barber was called a coward for fleeing.

In the last year of *The Voice of the Negro*, the magazine gave up all pretense of being fair and balanced in its reporting. The magazine openly supported Du Bois's new Niagara Movement, and Barber, like many other critics of Washington, became one of its founding members. Washington never eased up on him and continued to attack his character whenever he could. Eventually Barber left journalism for other occupations, only to find Washington's influence hovering over his attempts to obtain a job. Finally he studied to become a dentist. He ran a successful dental practice in Philadelphia, and Washington quit bothering him. As Louis Harlan concluded, "Contrary to the fable, the giant overcame the would-be giant killer." Eventually the tables would be turned on Washington, but his extensive and clandestine control of the black press was a powerful element of his program and showed the lengths he would go to silence his critics. Scott and Fortune, in letters to each other, would sometimes refer to Washington as "the Wizard." Washington at times seemed to possess almost unlimited, often disguised powers to control his own destiny and shape his empire. Like the Wizard of Oz in the movie version, though, his critics were beginning to see the man behind the curtain.

In his quest for power, Washington also created institutions where they did not exist. In 1900 he called for the establishment of a National Negro Business League to bring together black businessmen and women from around the country for information and inspiration. Washington held the first meeting in Boston with representatives from twenty-five states, including a large Southern representation. The membership reflected the nature of black business in America, which consisted mainly of individual shop owners and tradesmen. Washington proudly listed them by occupation in *The Story of My Life and Work*. "They represented many of the commercial enterprises in which white men are engaged," he wrote. "There were among them bankers, real estate dealers, grocers, dry goods merchants, caterers, manufacturers, contractors, druggists, undertakers, bakers, restaurant keepers, barbers, printers, plumbers, milliners, dressmakers, jewelers, publishers, and farmers."

The National Negro Business League represented one of the main pillars of Washington's philosophy: once an education had been acquired, it was important to get a job in order to become economically independent. Ultimate independence would be land ownership, home ownership, and ownership of one's own business whenever possible. Business success was the ultimate test of success in America, for any American regardless of race. Many of the businessmen and women who attended that first meeting represented small businesses in all-black towns or in segregated sections of Southern cities. Many were barely making ends meet, often operating in poor communities and catering mostly to a black clientele. But others came from large Northern cities and from the West, where businesses were small but not necessarily subjected to Jim Crow practices.

The goal of the Business League was to promote self-help and financial success. Washington was elected president,· and virtually all the officers and executive committee members were his supporters. Fortune was prominent on the executive committee. Funding to create the Business League came from Andrew Carnegie, with additional support over the years from John D. Rockefeller, Jr., John Wanamaker, and other white industrialists and merchants who had befriended Washington. At the first meeting William Lloyd Garrison, Jr., son of the famed abolitionist, spoke about the importance of land ownership and business ownership as roads to independence. He urged the members to pay off the mortgages on their homes and be free of debt. "Independence and debt cannot long keep company," he said.

The National Negro Business League was composed of branches of local leagues scattered across the country and eventually included hundreds of chapters. More than twelve hundred delegates attended the 1912 annual meeting in Atlanta. The organization gave Washington a powerful network of supporters who were prominent in the lives of their communities. The members of the Business League could serve as eyes and ears for the news Washington needed to keep his finger on the pulse of black communities across the nation.

The league's programs, as the historian August Meier pointed out, represented two conflicting ideas that Washington hoped would be reconciled over time. The league always championed the conservative business view that laissez-faire economics would work for blacks as well as it worked for whites. In other words, the business marketplace was color blind. A citrus grower from Florida observed that no one cared what color the grower was as long as the oranges and grapefruit were fresh and ripe. Washington believed that blacks would succeed in a free-market economy if given a chance. On the other hand, the purpose of the league was to support and promote black-owned businesses—an economic black nationalism that ran counter to the notion of a color-blind market. Race prejudice in business was evidently on the mind of some of the members who spoke at various conventions even while they offered stories that supported the free-market idea.

In Jim Crow America the fact was that the market was not free. Some of the most successful local chapters of the league had aggressive programs that encouraged blacks to buy from black businesses. The league's full-time organizer, Fred R. Moore, put it bluntly when he said, "Jews support Jews, Germans support Germans; Italians support Italians until they get strong enough to compete with their brothers in the professions and trades; and Negroes should now begin to support Negroes." Ironically, as Jim Crow conditions worsened in America, some black businesses—especially barbering—lost their former white customers and had to rely more on black clients.

The boosterism of the National Negro Business League had its positive side in promoting black business but ultimately suffered the fate of Washington's overall emphasis on positive thinking, which sometimes flew in the face of reality. As long as black business was constrained by the color line, it would be doomed by limitations that prevented economic independence. It was true that a few blacks made fortunes and became millionaires, but usually they appealed exclusively to black customers. Most prominent at the time was Madam C. J. Walker, who developed a line of cosmetics and hair preparations for black women. Born Sarah Breedlove in Louisiana in 1867, she worked as a washerwoman and cook before getting into the cosmetic business, where she found a niche that white business was not serving. It was the kind of business that could succeed in segregated America. Walker employed a small army of agents who made good money selling her products in black communities. When she died in 1919 she left money to both Tuskegee Institute and the NAACP.

Washington's widening sphere of influence with organizations, black churches, and newspapers gave him the ability to act through agents. An early example was his work through the Afro-American Council to fight disfranchisement in New Orleans and to push a court case to test Louisiana's grandfather clause that kept blacks from the polls. If blacks could prove that their grandfathers had the franchise, they would be allowed to vote. But since most blacks voting in the 1890s were descended from slaves who did not have the right to vote, the grandfather clause was tantamount to disfranchisement.

In the New Orleans case Washington worked in complete secrecy, cautioning activists in New Orleans never to use his name. He raised money for the test case from white philanthropists and put up some of his own money. The Afro-American Council books showed his entries as being from "X.Y.Z." After four years this legal effort went nowhere. Washington blamed it on wrangling in the committee of local lawyers. Washington then turned his attention to several Alabama cases and hired his own personal lawyer, Wilford H. Smith, to handle them. To keep correspondence between Smith and Emmett Scott from falling into the wrong hands, they used the fictitious names R. C. Black and J. C. May. Smith also used "McAdoo" occasionally while Washington was called "His Nibs." It was unacceptable for Washington to be connected with these court challenges on behalf of black voters. The public Washington, the exemplary citizen, received a lifetime voting certificate from the state of Alabama, which he hung in his home.

In other secret cases that challenged railroad segregation and other Jim Crow laws in Georgia, Tennessee, and Virginia, Washington directed the action behind the scenes and provided money for lawyers. He even worked secretly with W. E. B. Du Bois against a 1902 Georgia law that provided for segregated railroad sleeping cars. This did not stop Du Bois from publicly breaking with Washington's leadership the following year.

Washington was successful in his secret activities to fight a particularly insidious form of slavery called peonage, or debt slavery, in a case that went all the way to the Supreme Court. It was about an Alabama farmhand named Alonzo Bailey who in 1907 signed a contract to work for $12 a month. He then borrowed $15 on future wages, which he was to repay at the rate of $1.25 a month taken from his wages. Bailey worked several months under this arrangement and then quit his job. The fact that he left his employer with a debt unpaid was considered under Alabama's peonage law to be prima facie evidence that Bailey had committed fraud on a contract. He would be sentenced to work on a chain gang. The peonage statute virtually gave any white man who claimed that a black man owed him money the right to bring charges against the debtor; in the event of conviction, the punishment was forced labor. Until the Alonzo Bailey case, however, there had been no challenge in the courts to test the constitutionality of the peonage law.

Washington used all his influence with sympathetic Alabama judges, and through his close ties to President Theodore Roosevelt he enlisted the support of Attorney General Charles J. Bonaparte. The challenge to the Alabama supreme court ended with the court upholding the peonage law as a means of controlling fraud. The case was then appealed to the U.S. Supreme Court. When the first effort before that Court failed, the challenge had to be renewed. By this time Roosevelt was out of office, and Washington had to enlist a new cast of characters, including a new attorney general to push the case again.

Washington worked hard on the Bailey case for years, enlisting donors, calling on his Northern associates like Oswald Garrison Villard, editor of the *New York Evening Post*, and many others. Finally, in 1911 the high court overturned the peonage statute as an unconstitutional form of involuntary servitude. It was Washington's last major effort to finance and push civil rights issues secretly. Halfway through the case, in 1909, the NAACP was founded and became the major vehicle for challenging Jim Crow in the courts. The NAACP operated openly while Washington's role remained invisible to the public.

As far as the public knew, Washington was true to his public pledge of 1895 not to agitate for civil rights. He successfully maintained his secrecy. Behind closed doors, however, he was doing just the opposite. He may have fooled a good many white people in the South by his actions, and kept his leadership intact by not provoking Southern sentiments on civil rights. But Washington's secrecy cost him dearly in the support of many blacks who were growing impatient with worsening conditions and the slow pace of progress under his leadership.

Even the Supreme Court decision in the Bailey case did not halt peonage in other parts of the South. The NAACP was cool to the idea of pursuing other peonage cases; it had a different agenda. As Pete Daniel explained in his book on peonage, *The Shadow of Slavery*, peonage persisted in the backwaters of the South long after Booker T. Washington was gone. Cases continued to be reported into the 1940s. It was a dastardly aspect of the sharecropping system that dominated Southern agriculture even after the mule had been replaced by the tractor. Slavery died hard. Nothing that Washington did in secret, even when court challenges were successful, seemed to slow down the scourge of Jim Crow. Never one to exhibit public discouragement, Washington's response was to throw himself even harder into his work, redoubling both his public utterances in support of his program and his efforts behind the scenes to combat his critics.

There had never been a black leader like Booker T. Washington, nor a national network of both public and clandestine activities on behalf of black advancement like the Tuskegee Machine that Washington assembled by sheer will and a never-ending attention to details. There is no evidence that he ever doubted the wisdom of his program or the practical efficiency of the network he assembled. He was convinced that his plan and his work, even his assault on his enemies and critics, were in the best interests of his race.

CHAPTER SEVEN

Two Warring Ideals

I do not believe that politics in the South will be divided on race lines much longer.—Booker T. Washington, interviewed in 1897

. . . The problem of the Twentieth Century is the problem of the color-line.—W. E. B. Du Bois, *The Souls of Black Folk*, 1903

꙳   Booker T. Washington had critics before he was launched to national fame in 1895, but they seemed scattered and of no consequence. At first they appeared to be crackpots and malcontents who were easily dismissed. But like a trickling stream that grows to be a powerful river, criticism of Washington's leadership grew steadily over the years until it became a raging torrent when he was at the very height of his power, in the opening years of the twentieth century. For the last dozen years of his life he would cling to power and in all outward appearances remain the most famous and influential black man in America. But his leadership eroded rapidly. He became a polarizing figure—leader of a faction, not of a people.

The assault on Washington's leadership came from many quarters. White supremacists attacked him regularly as their favorite and most prominent black whipping boy. Thomas Heflin, a race-baiting lawyer and Alabama congressman, seldom missed a chance to attack Washington on matters

large or small. Heflin used the incident of Washington's dining with President Roosevelt at the White House to whip
up support in his 1904 election campaign, when he quipped
that had an anarchist thrown a bomb under the table where
Washington and Roosevelt were dining, "no harm would
have been done."

Washington had put up with this brand of criticism his
whole career. His racist critics were not confined to the
South: a prominent white attorney, Edward Morris, a Republican assistant state's attorney in Cook County, Illinois, and
past grand master of the Odd Fellows lodge, told the Chicago
Inter Ocean following a gruesome lynching in Danville, Illinois, in 1903, "Booker T. Washington is largely responsible
for the lynching in this country." He went on to say that
"The learned doctor teaches the colored people that they are
only fit to fill menial positions. The spirit of his teaching is
illustrated by a rag-time song, 'Mr. Coon, You're All Right
in Your Place.'" Morris said he preferred a radical like Senator Benjamin Tillman of South Carolina who "comes out
openly and attacks negroes and condones lynching."

Washington generally ignored such assaults and did not
dignify them with a response. But he could not ignore the
growing chorus of his black critics. In Jim Crow America
it was one thing to be ridiculed by white leaders who made
political capital by promoting white supremacy; it was far
more threatening to Washington for blacks to attack him for
leading them in the wrong direction. This was a direct challenge to his program and his leadership. Change was in the
air as the new century began. How Washington responded to
his black critics would define his leadership.

The nation was in the midst of a major political realign-
ment in the opening decade of the twentieth century. The
ideals of the Progressive Era affected both major political parties and included an array of reforms designed to promote

good government: regulation of business and industry, an end to monopolistic practices, pure food and drug reform, better wages and working conditions for laborers, improved housing and tenement reform, and a variety of social programs directed toward the vast numbers of immigrants flooding into America. Newspapers exposed corrupt practices; magazines ran exposés of all kinds, including one that accused the U.S. Senate of treason because it was controlled by special interests known as trusts, which bribed senators to support their interests. Upton Sinclair published *The Jungle*, which dealt with the problems faced by immigrant workers in the meatpacking industry. Jacob Riis took his camera, a relatively new tool for journalists, into the New York slums and revealed lives of poverty and squalor never before seen by most Americans in his book *How the Other Half Lives*. Journalists who dug into corruption were labeled "muckrakers" by President Roosevelt, a term that stuck and became a badge of honor to those who saw their work as exposing evils in society.

This broad spirit of journalistic investigation with the hope of reform also affected thinking on race relations, at least among blacks and some of their white allies in the North. In the aftermath of the Atlanta Riot of 1906, the journalist Ray Stannard Baker traveled through the nation, exploring the effects of Jim Crow in America with articles in the pages of *McClure's* and the *American Magazine*. A book version, *Following the Color Line*, was published in 1908. It remains the best journalistic account of race relations in America in the opening years of the twentieth century. Baker investigated the Atlanta Riot, lynching, racial attitudes, and blacks in politics. He interviewed prominent white and black leaders across the country, including Washington and Du Bois as well as white supremacists like Tillman and James K. Vardaman. Baker uncovered a great deal of racism but offered no solution to the vexing problem other than to improve understanding between the races. "Two elements appear in every race problem," he wrote, "the first, race prejudice—the repulsion of the unlike; second, economic or competitive jealousy."

Baker saw in stark terms that there were "Two Great Negro Parties," two distinct factions of black thought and race leadership, one headed by Washington and the other by Du Bois. Baker wrote, "Nothing has been more remarkable in the recent history of the Negro than Washington's rise to influence as a leader, and the spread of his ideals of education and progress." Baker saw black leadership in regional terms: Washington represented the South, Du Bois the North. "The party led by Washington is made up of the masses of the common people," he wrote; "the radical party, on the other hand, represents what may be called the intellectuals." Baker described Du Bois as the leader of a minority party that was "torn with dissention and discontent."

The major Progressive reforms led by Theodore Roosevelt and later Woodrow Wilson failed to address the concerns of black Americans. But within the black communities there was talk of a "New Negro for a New Century." Some of these ideas would gel after Washington's death and emerge in the 1920s in a remarkable cultural outpouring known as the Harlem Renaissance. In Washington's lifetime the broad wave of Progressive reform manifested itself among blacks and their white allies as a new push for civil rights. In this respect the Progressive challenge to racial injustice was in conflict with Washington's accommodationist position on civil rights. He sought to discourage social and political agitation while the Progressives looked for corruption and unfairness with a new sense of moral urgency. Progressive reforms largely ignored black America in the South, but black intellectuals in the North were among the first to be attracted to the movement.

While Du Bois epitomized the challenge to Washington's leadership, it was Du Bois's friend, William Monroe Trotter, who led the early assault on him. As a Northern intellectual critic of Washington, the fiery, iconoclastic black newspaper editor from Boston broke sharply with the man from Tuskegee. Trotter made his reputation as a passionate, no-holds-barred opponent. His family background and education were in stark contrast to Washington's humble origins. Called Monroe, Trotter had been born in 1872 in Ohio. He was almost a full generation younger than Washington. Trotter's father James, born a slave in Mississippi in 1842, later served with distinction in the Civil War in the all-black Fifty-fifth Massachusetts Regiment, one of whose white officers was none other than the son of the abolitionist William Lloyd Garrison, a connection that cemented a relationship between the two families. James Trotter would later be named recorder of deeds in Washington, D.C., by President Grover Cleveland. The family lived for a while in the white community of Hyde Park in Chicago and then moved to Boston, where Monroe Trotter graduated magna cum laude in the Harvard class of 1895 and earned a master's degree from Harvard the following year. He was the first black man to be awarded a Phi Beta Kappa key. In November 1901 he co-founded the black newspaper the *Boston Guardian* and began publishing from the same building that had been the home of William Lloyd Garrison's prominent abolitionist paper, *The Liberator.*

Trotter early set his sights on Booker T. Washington and used the pages of his weekly newspaper to lambaste Washington's conservative leadership, especially his compromise with the South to avoid political and social agitation. Trotter demanded civil rights and political rights, and anyone who might stand in the way of these goals was grist for his mill. The *Guardian* challenged the newspapers that Washington

William Monroe Trotter, editor of the *Boston Guardian*, was a harsh critic of Washington and a leading member of the Talented Tenth.

either owned or subsidized, and its editorials were often countered in the pages of black newspapers under Washington's control.

Booker Washington and Monroe Trotter were like oil and water. Washington, the industrial-school-trained, mild-mannered conciliator from the South found his opposite in Trotter, the Harvard-educated militant protester from Hyde Park and Boston. Trotter despised Washington's accommodation to Jim Crow. In an editorial in December 1902 he questioned how Washington could remain silent while Southern states wrote new constitutions that disfranchised blacks and further strengthened the barriers that confined blacks to second-class status. Trotter asked, "what man is a worse enemy to a race than a leader who looks with equanimity on the disfranchisement of his race in a country where other races have universal suffrage by constitutions that make one rule for his race and another for the dominant race . . . ?" A few months later, in early 1903, another Trotter editorial decried Washington's constant admonition against agitation for rights: "This habit of belittling agitation on the part of Washington, that very thing which made him free, and by which he lives and prospers is one of his great faults. . . ."

Washington of course considered Trotter a troublemaker and an extremist. At first he followed the advice of his friend T. Thomas Fortune to ignore Trotter and "let the whole gang howl." But Trotter's attacks persisted, and Washington found himself spending more time finding ways to answer or neutralize his critics. This internecine warfare, conducted through the pages of black newspapers, revealed a sharp polarization of black thought on the future advancement of the race and who should lead it. The ideological struggle was intensified by deteriorating racial conditions across the country, which neither side seemed able to overcome. Jim Crow was creeping into the North. It was quickly becoming a national, not just a regional, problem.

As critics like Trotter accelerated their attacks, Washington began to see his college-educated critics in stereotypical terms that aroused the old anti-intellectual feelings he had harbored throughout his life. College-educated blacks like Trotter and W. E. B. Du Bois, he wrote, "know books but they do not know men . . . they understand theories, but they do not understand things." Trotter in fact was a terrible intellectual snob who snubbed everything that wasn't Boston or Harvard. His style and behavior reinforced Washington's negative view of him.

The two men bonded through aversion. Washington and his lieutenants desperately tried to undermine and discredit Trotter and his newspaper while Trotter plotted and schemed to expose Washington's lust for power and his attempts to be the dictator of race leadership. One of Trotter's goals was to get white newspapers to take notice of the criticism in the black press of Washington's leadership. On one occasion Trotter tried to disrupt a meeting in St. Louis where Washington was speaking, hoping it would be covered in the white newspapers, but the attempt fell short. Most white papers simply were not interested.

The Washington/Trotter imbroglio reached a peak in the so-called Boston Riot on the evening of July 30, 1903. It was not a riot by any stretch of the imagination, but that is how the press characterized it and how it has been labeled ever since. More important, it was the first major public incident where criticism of Washington's leadership made headlines in both white and black newspapers. The white-run *Boston Globe* began its lengthy coverage of the event: "Surrounded by a struggling mass of angry people of his own race, in the confusion of fainting women and fighting men, unable to address his audience or to persuade them into a state of sanity, Booker T. Washington met his first really hostile demonstration in Boston last evening at the Zion A.M.E. church. . . ."

On that warm July evening, the Columbus Avenue A.M.E. Zion Church was packed to the rafters with people who had come to hear Washington, the featured speaker. Monroe Trotter had made sure the audience included plenty of anti-Bookerites. When the master of ceremonies, William H. Lewis, another black Harvard man, mentioned Washington's name, loud hissing began. A minister admonished the audience that there should be no hissing in a house of God. Lewis, a famous football player and assistant U.S. district attorney, threatened to call in the police unless the hecklers quieted down. "If there are any geese in the audience," he said, "they are privileged to retire." But this pronouncement led to more hissing, outbursts, and sporadic demonstrations against Washington.

Finally, T. Thomas Fortune was able to speak on behalf of Washington and introduce him. He spoke just a few sentences before he began to cough and sneeze uncontrollably. Other speakers on the platform, including Washington, also began sneezing and coughing. Someone had spread cayenne pepper all over the stage and podium. After Fortune regained his composure and finished his remarks, one of the agitators, Granville Martin of Boston, a friend of Trotter's, was ordered out of the church, and police were called in to remove him. At this point Trotter himself leaped to his feet and yelled, "Put me out, arrest me." Trotter had come prepared to cause trouble; he had a list of nine accusatory questions for Washington. The ruckus escalated even as the program proceeded. The prominent black singer Harry Burleigh sang, calming the audience temporarily.

Trying to remain calm through the disruptions, Washington took the podium and began to speak. Jostling and unrest in the church continued. Washington completed his remarks, but not before there were hostile shouts from the audience. Trotter jumped onto a chair and read his prepared questions but was drowned out in the shouting. Among his questions for Washington were the following: "Don't you know you would help the race more by exposing the new form of slavery [sharecropping] just outside the gates of Tuskegee than by preaching submission? Can a man make a successful educator and politician at the same time? Is the rope and the torch all the race is to get under your leadership?"

Police now entered the church, causing further confusion. Several women fainted, one person was slashed with a razor, another was stuck with a hat pin, and a man had his jacket ripped open. The police arrested Trotter, his sister, and several others; they were handcuffed and led out as the meeting continued. Washington, shaken to the core, remained outwardly calm. After his talk he greeted the many well-wishers in the audience who pressed forward to shake his hand. To the *Boston Globe* he sought to minimize the disturbance: "Just as a few flies are able to impair the purity of a jar of cream, so three or four ill-mannered young colored men were able to disturb an otherwise successful meeting of the colored citizens of Boston tonight."

Trotter was found guilty of disturbing the peace and served a month in jail; charges against the others were dropped. Trotter found himself roundly condemned in the white press as a troublemaker, as he was in the black newspapers under Washington's control. But he came out of this staged event with exactly what he had hoped to achieve. He made a breakthrough to the white press, making them aware that some blacks did not follow Booker T. Washington's line. Washington, on the other hand, used the opportunity to further discredit Trotter. An anonymous news release, secretly prepared by Emmett Scott, revealed the Tuskegee Machine at work smearing Trotter by suggesting he had gone insane in his opposition to Washington and that he had employed prostitutes to help disrupt the meeting. Washington told his many supporters that Trotter's behavior had ruined him as a serious, influential commentator on racial issues.

Washington had far better relations with his most important black critic, W. E. B. Du Bois, but in the end it was Du Bois, not Monroe Trotter, who had the greatest impact on Washington's leadership. As with Trotter, the personal differences between Washington and Du Bois in temperament, style, and outlook were remarkable. Often they have been portrayed as polar opposites of black thought at the beginning of the twentieth century. The views and actions of these two men would set much of the tone for the racial dialogue of their time and into the future. In many respects their backgrounds, educational achievements, and priorities for racial advancement were indeed in sharp contrast, but they differed primarily on the importance of civil rights and open protest against racial injustice. This was a gulf that Washington could not bridge.

Washington and Du Bois had in common a yearning for an education, even though their paths took vastly different directions. Du Bois had graduated from Fisk University in 1888 and then attended Harvard, where he received a bachelor's degree cum laude in 1890. He then studied at Berlin University in Germany and became the first black American to receive a Ph.D. from Harvard, in 1895, the same year that Washington gave his Atlanta Address. With his limited formal education and his honorary master's degree from Harvard, Washington could not hope to match Du Bois's academic resumé. Twelve years younger than Washington, Du Bois had been born in Great Barrington, Massachusetts, in 1868, in a small town about 135 miles west of Boston in the Housatonic River Valley in the Berkshire Hills. He was of mixed ancestry, including French Huguenots, and was light complected. His father abandoned him and his mother when he was two years old, and they lived in poverty. Du Bois worked as a child and excelled in school, where he was encouraged to study the classics. He was one of the few black children in the area. He did not feel different from the other children until a white girl refused to play with him because he was black.

While Washington worked in the South and built a normal and industrial school from scratch, Du Bois was building a firm foundation as one of the leading black academics and intellectuals in America. He did research for his classic sociological study, *The Philadelphia Negro* (1899), while teaching at the University of Pennsylvania, and he taught at Wilberforce College and Clark University in Atlanta (later Clark Atlanta University).

William Edward Burghardt Du Bois, the leading black intellectual of Washington's time, was his chief critic. Du Bois founded the Niagara Movement, developed the concept of the Talented Tenth, and was a founder and leader of the NAACP. *(Library of Congress)*

The two men grew farther apart in style and substance until they represented two distinct approaches to race advancement. Washington clung to his philosophy that industrial education was the best road to advancement for the masses of black Americans. Tuskegee Institute was his showcase for this type of education. Du Bois, Harvard educated and academically inclined, believed that the best hope for the future of the race lay in what he called the Talented Tenth, the top 10 percent of black Americans who could gain a college education and enter the professions, where they would be the most effective leaders in promoting racial advancement. This group of college-educated black professionals included journalists, editors, ministers, lawyers, and educators.

Among the outstanding members of the Talented Tenth was John Hope of Atlanta Baptist College, who urged blacks not to be satisfied with Jim Crow and to push for political and social rights. Hope's example showed that it was possible to be bold even in the South. But his strident voice was an exception to others of the Talented Tenth in the South. Washington, D.C., a Southern town with a cosmopolitan element, was filled with members of the Talented Tenth, led by J. W. Cromwell, a school principal who supported Booker T. Washington early on and then switched allegiances. In the North the Talented Tenth existed in cities like New York, Boston, Philadelphia, and Chicago. In Boston, Du Bois's fellow Harvard man Monroe Trotter fit the mold. A Baltimore group was led by Mason A. Hawkins, a schoolteacher who later joined Du Bois's Niagara Movement. Considering there were about ten million blacks in the United States in 1900, the Talented Tenth actually amounted to closer to 1 percent, not 10 percent, of the black population. The black professional class of college-educated men and women would double by 1910 but still represent less than 3 percent of the black population. Nonetheless Du Bois saw this group's potential influence as much greater than their numbers.

Washington was never opposed to the concept of the Talented Tenth as an educational theory or as a pool of talent from which to draw future leaders. He often spoke in favor of higher education for blacks, but he always tempered his remarks with a caution that higher education was fine for some but not most blacks. He was concerned about the masses of black Americans who had neither the means nor the preparation to earn advanced degrees from prestigious institutions. Washington was concerned with the 99 percent who needed to learn to read and write, to learn enough arithmetic to run businesses, and to gain skills for much-needed jobs as bricklayers, carpenters, dressmakers, milliners, and other practical occupations. Washington's plan was to fight the poverty and ignorance he saw in the Black Belt of Alabama and elsewhere, where basic hygiene and the use of a toothbrush ranked far higher on the agenda of priorities than gaining a Harvard education.

What Washington distrusted about the Talented Tenth was that college-educated blacks formed an anti-Bookerite movement. They were a threat to his leadership. He was leery of the Talented Tenth in the same way he earlier had expressed discomfort with intellectuals and preachers who passed themselves off as "doctors." While Du Bois was the genuine article—an accomplished, talented, academically trained intellectual—Washington believed he was out of touch with the masses. Du Bois liked to dress the part of the academic dandy. His clothes, his walking stick, and the spats he wore marked him as a college man. His haughty style, academic pretensions, and aloofness all had their effect on Washington's estimate of this Harvard man.

Washington the politician knew he had to find a way to control Du Bois and the Talented Tenth. The two men were not unfriendly toward each other, even as their rivalry grew. Du Bois knew Washington's third wife Margaret from their days at Fisk University together. Earlier Du Bois had complimented Washington on the Atlanta Address. However grudgingly, they interacted in numerous ways, both publicly and privately. In 1903 Du Bois was actually teaching summer school at Tuskegee and dining with Washington in his home, The Oaks, on the campus following the publication of Du Bois's scathing attack on Washington's leadership.

Du Bois and his followers were rapidly becoming obstacles to Washington's political dominance within the black community. Their willingness to speak out on racial injustice also threatened Washington's delicately maintained compromise with the white South. As criticism of Washington's gradualist approach to race advancement grew, it became harder for Washington to sell his program to blacks and more difficult for him to justify his dominance of black Republican politics in the South. For the remaining twelve years of his life, he would never lose power completely, but he found that he had to work harder to retain it while employing Machiavellian methods to keep his critics in check. When Washington's opponents hardened into enemies, he redoubled his efforts to defeat them. By 1903, eight years after the Atlanta Address, Washington's Tuskegee Machine and his clandestine efforts to fight Jim Crow had turned inward to protect his own power. He spent more time combating the rise of the Talented Tenth and more time answering his critics than he did fighting Jim Crow.

In 1903, with the publication of Du Bois's masterful book *The Souls of Black Folk*, things would never be quite the same for Washington. Du Bois's manifesto was an idea whose time had come, even if Washington was slow to see it. *The Souls of Black Folk* was destined to become one of the most inspirational and insightful expositions on race ever written. But in its own time, in Jim Crow America, the most striking thing about the book was an essay "On Booker T. Washington and Others," which laid down the gauntlet and defined the forthcoming struggle against Washington's leadership. Du Bois began his essay by recognizing Washington's ascent to power, calling it "easily the most striking thing in the history of the Negro since 1876." Du Bois understood the context of Washington's success and how his program of industrial education and soft-pedaling of civil rights seemed right for the times. Washington's single-minded adherence to industrial education and gradual economic advancement had won him many friends and followers as well as personal success and prosperity. "It is," Du Bois wrote, "as though Nature must needs make men narrow in order to give them force."

By 1903 Du Bois demonstrated how far he had moved away from Washington, whom he saw as a cult figure. He looked with disfavor on the Atlanta Address, which he branded "the Atlanta Compromise." He took a hard look at Washington's leadership and found it wanting in a number of particulars. Despite Washington's popularity, Du Bois wrote, his network of contacts, his acceptance and financial support from prominent white captains of industry, and his influence with the president of the United States, within the black community there was growing resentment of his leadership. ". . . [T]here is among educated and thoughtful colored men in all parts of the land a feeling of deep regret, sorrow, and apprehension at the wide currency and ascendency which some of Mr. Washington's theories have gained."

Du Bois did not question Washington's sincerity, his hard work, or his dedication, and acknowledged that in many ways he retained the "respect of all." Still Du Bois launched a list of grievances: Washington tried to silence his critics and inhibit a healthy dialogue. He represented an old style of leadership of "adjustment and submission." His program focused on work and money, which "overshadowed the higher aims of life." Du Bois charged, "Mr. Washington's programme practically accepts the alleged inferiority of the Negro races."

The failure of Washington's strategy, according to Du Bois, could be seen in the results of his "tender of the palm-branch" to the white South. Blacks had been disfranchised and placed in a "distinct status of civil inferiority," and aid to higher education had fallen in favor of support for industrial education. Du Bois did not blame Washington for all these setbacks, but he did assert that Washington's "propaganda" had "helped their speedier accomplishment." His program and his leadership now faced a dire situation and a paradox. Washington had trained blacks for jobs but had not given them the tools to defend their rights, namely the right to vote. Du Bois's critique ends with a call to oppose part of Washington's program and leadership.

> So far as Mr. Washington preaches Thrift, Patience, and Industrial training for the masses, we must hold up his hands and strive with him, rejoicing in his honors and glorying in the strength of this Joshua called of God and man to lead the headless host. But so far as Mr. Washington apologizes for injustice, North or South, does not rightly value the privilege and duty of voting, belittles the emasculating effects of caste distinctions, and opposes higher training and ambition of our brighter minds—so far as he, the South, or the Nation, does this—we must unceasingly and firmly oppose them. By every civilized and peaceful method we must strive for the rights which the world accords to men, clinging unwaveringly to those great words which the sons of the Fathers would fain forget: "We hold these truths to be self-evident: That all men are created equal; that they are endowed by their Creator with certain unalienable rights; that among these are life, liberty, and the pursuit of happiness."

This signal essay shows how quickly circumstances were changing for Washington even when he enjoyed the height of his influence. Du Bois's views were an expression of the new Progressive Era as it applied to black Americans. The worsening conditions of Jim Crow America called for a new approach. They demanded racial justice and a frontal assault on disfranchisement and racial discrimination. Du

Bois tried to compromise with Washington in recognizing the good he had accomplished. Du Bois did not completely repudiate him. But his olive branch was a small one. He would not compromise on the struggle against racial injustice; it was time to be more vigorous in the war against the Jim Crow system. Thus Du Bois made the transition from scholar to activist, as the historian Manning Marable put it. Washington never made that transition. He remained a public educator and private political boss but never made the leap to protest.

Washington was incapable of heeding Du Bois's warning. He had invested too much in his own program. He was a success, he had power, he had influence. He would not yield to his critics, no matter how eloquent they might be. Nor would he jeopardize his school, his influence, or his power by abandoning his conservative gradualism. He had too much at stake to adjust to changing times, and he was not convinced Du Bois was right. Washington could not be the man to lead a frontal assault on Jim Crow when his whole life was based on finding ways to accommodate to it while building within a racially closed system.

Washington dismissed Du Bois's essay and used the occasion of the publication of *The Souls of Black Folk* to encourage his friends and lieutenants, especially those at black newspapers he controlled, to make sure reviews of the book contained a justification of Washington's program. *The Outlook*, one of the leading journals of the day, did just that in its review, which contained several paragraphs in defense of Washington. One of Washington's supporters, H. T. Burleigh, a leading black musician in New York, wrote to Washington that "a blind man can see that Du Bois's work is purely personal whereas yours is general: you are for the masses while he pleads for the classes. It is obvious who has the greater and higher field."

Washington and Du Bois engaged in a delicate dance with each other for several tense years. Washington looked for ways to work with Du Bois, but always on his own terms. Du Bois, like so many others in the Talented Tenth, recognized Washington's power and influence as a race leader but became increasingly frustrated with his heavy-handed politics, which he viewed as dictatorial. Du Bois saw clearly that Washington was not willing to go beyond the strictures he had set down for himself and his race in the Atlanta Address.

The last significant effort by both men to seek common ground came at a major conference held at Carnegie Hall in New York City, January 6–8, 1904. Washington had thought of organizing such a conference earlier, but in the aftermath of the Boston Riot and Du Bois's indictment of his leadership in *The Souls of Black Folk* such a conference took on a new urgency. Washington realized that his power was slipping and that he needed to regain control.

The plan, worked out in the second half of 1903, was to invite a small group of prominent thinkers on race who reflected a spectrum of thought. Washington consulted with Du Bois, assuring him that "the meeting not be confined to those who agree with my own views regarding education and the position which the race shall assume in public affairs." Despite these assurances, Washington stacked the deck and made sure the blacks who were present were mostly Bookerites.

It took months of behind-the-scenes maneuvering just to arrange the list of those invited. The negotiations were secret, but news of the conference leaked out. Monroe Trotter, who was not invited, used the pages of the *Boston Guardian* to gossip about the forthcoming meeting. The number of those invited grew to twenty-seven blacks, with a half-day set aside for presentations from white leaders invited by

Washington. Du Bois hoped this conference would provide him an opportunity to set forth his own agenda, which he presented in a letter to Kelly Miller of Howard University. Foremost on Du Bois's list was "Full political rights on the same terms as other Americans." He sought higher education for "selected Negro youth" and industrial education "for the masses." He rounded out his program with a need to stop "the campaign of self-deprecation" and to create a defense fund for court challenges of civil rights violations. He wanted more study of the conditions of black life in America, closer cooperation among black societies, and the creation of a national journal on black issues.

When Du Bois saw the list of those who would attend the Carnegie Hall Conference, he recognized that he had been outmaneuvered. Two-thirds of the attendees were Washington supporters. Tempers grew short especially following the appearance of prominent white journalists, educators, and philanthropists who paraded in and spoke of Washington in glowing terms. Andrew Carnegie himself attended, having footed the bill for the event. The conference solved nothing. It only added to the growing polarization among those working for race advancement. Washington, on the other hand, believed it was a success. It had afforded him an opportunity to size up his opposition, and he felt confident he could control and minimize the influence of the anti-Bookerites.

The resolutions that came out of the conference encompassed some of Du Bois's agenda, but they were diluted. The conference set in motion the creation of a Committee of Twelve for the Advancement of the Negro Race, which would carry forth ideas proposed at the conference. Again Du Bois was outmaneuvered in the selection of the committee. Washington, Du Bois, and Hugh M. Browne, principal of the Institute for Colored Youth in Pennsylvania, were named as an executive committee to select the other nine members of the Committee of Twelve. Browne turned out to be a Bookerite. Browne and Washington thus selected members who favored Washington's leadership, including Washington's close friend T. Thomas Fortune.

Although Andrew Carnegie funded the Committee of Twelve with an annual contribution of $2,700, it was little more than a paper organization. The committee helped with a disfranchisement case in Maryland in 1905 but otherwise proved ineffective. It continued to exist for almost a decade. By 1910, however, it decided to convert its small amount of cash into a publishing venture to produce an annual Negro Yearbook. Washington hired Monroe Work to compile the volume, with Tuskegee Institute as a partner in the enterprise. Du Bois quickly drifted away from the work of the Committee of Twelve and missed its first meeting in St. Louis in 1904 supposedly due to illness. Others who were tired of Washington's leadership tendered their resignations early on.

Washington and his ever-present secretary Emmett Scott believed they had neutralized Du Bois after the Carnegie Hall Conference. Scott wrote to Washington that he was glad Du Bois had missed the first meeting of the Committee of Twelve. Scott thought Du Bois "has all but decided to flock by himself. I think he will be practically harmless from now on." Du Bois was indeed ready to go his own way. He had a new organization in mind, one that would not be under the thumb of Booker T. Washington.

CHAPTER EIGHT

Niagara's Mighty Waters

What does civilization owe the negro? Nothing! Nothing!
NOTHING!—Hoke Smith, during his campaign for governor of
Georgia, 1905

It is good to be permitted to live in an age when great, serious
and perplexing problems are to be met and solved. For my part
I would not care to live in an age when there was no weak
part of the human family to be helped up and no wrongs to be
righted. Through struggle only are great men and useful races
produced.—Booker T. Washington's Christmas greeting, 1906

𝕊 In 1905 W. E. B. Du Bois launched the Niagara Movement, a new organization that called for an aggressive assault on Jim Crow in America. The name of the group was
selected to indicate the powerful new currents of change
it expected to unleash. Du Bois called a secret meeting of
several dozen supporters in Buffalo, New York, where they
planned a larger meeting for July 11–13 that year. Fifty-nine
persons were invited to the first meeting of the Niagara
Movement; twenty-nine attended. The pervasiveness of Jim
Crow practices, even in the North, resulted in this group of
well-dressed, college-educated, professional black men being
denied lodging in a Buffalo hotel. Their meeting was moved
to the Canadian side of the river. Under the leadership of Du
Bois and Washington's nemesis from the Boston Riot, Mon-

roe Trotter, the meeting offered a striking alternative to the
Carnegie Hall Conference.

The Niagara group issued a declaration of rights that
never mentioned Washington by name but repudiated his
accommodation to Jim Crow practices and his unwilling-
ness to agitate for civil rights. The Niagara declarations
called for manhood suffrage for blacks, full civil rights, equal
opportunities to succeed in a world free of race prejudice,
justice in the courts, a halt to the dehumanizing effects of
the convict-lease system, an end to Jim Crow railroad cars,
denial of Negro inferiority, and recognition that racial discrimination was wrong. The declarations also called for an
end to the growing segregation of churches as an unchris-
tian act. In education the declarations advocated common
school training for all blacks, support for industrial education, and the need for higher education. To avoid these declarations being viewed as demands with no duties attached,
they concluded with a list of duties that all black citizens
should support:

> The duty to vote.
> The duty to respect the rights of others.
> The duty to work.
> The duty to obey the laws.
> The duty to be clean and orderly.
> The duty to send our children to school.
> The duty to respect ourselves, even as we respect others.

Washington had gotten wind of the Du Bois plans and
immediately went into action to gather intelligence on the
Niagara Movement. He sent one Tuskegee employee on a
sudden vacation to Niagara Falls to scout around. He employed a black lawyer, Clifford Plummer, to spy on the
meeting itself. Plummer's best work was in convincing the
local Associated Press office in Buffalo not to report news
of the meeting or its declarations. The Tuskegee Machine

A 1905 tourist studio photograph of members of the Niagara Movement. Du Bois is in the middle of the second row, in the white hat. *(University of Massachusetts)*

was successful in keeping coverage of the first meeting to a minimum.

But the second meeting of the Niagara Movement was impossible to keep out of the newspapers. Planned for Harpers Ferry, West Virginia, the site of John Brown's Raid, on the hundredth anniversary of Brown's birth in August 1906, the meeting drew a larger group of delegates and supporters. It was infiltrated by an even greater number of Washington's spies, including Richard T. Greener, a Harvard graduate, and a shady character named Melvin Jack Chissum, whom Washington had first employed in 1903 to spy on Monroe Trotter. Chissum would become a regular fixture in Washington's secret efforts to keep an eye on his critics, often meeting him on park benches in New York and in other cities to get his instructions. Sometimes the two men used code names in correspondence. Acting the role of the espionage agent to the hilt, including carrying a concealed weapon and occasionally wearing a bulletproof vest, the obsequious Chissum would sign his letters to Washington with flourishes such as "I am, Your obedient humble servant, Chissum, to do with as your Eminence desires, absolutely."

The Niagara Movement was never an effective organization, but its ideas were powerful. Du Bois had no ability to manage an organization; his strength lay in his ideas. The movement never had money; Washington had a stranglehold on most of the money coming from white philanthropists. Nonetheless the Niagara Movement represented the future. It recognized the need to protest and to launch a direct assault on Jim Crow. Racial conditions continued to deteriorate; Jim Crow laws persisted and spread; racial prejudice went unchecked and unchallenged. The lynching of blacks peaked in 1901 and 1902 but continued steadily for the rest of Washington's life as alarming examples of barbarous, lawless conduct that went unpunished. Race riots revealed tensions in cities in both the South and the North. Blacks in the rural South had been reduced to sharecropping and victimization by a convict-lease system that was thinly disguised slavery.

Washington had trapped himself when he delivered the Atlanta Address in 1895. He now was rapidly falling out of step with the times. He failed to understand the protests of the Talented Tenth, who he saw as rabble-rousers like Monroe Trotter instead of serious people who had given much thought to race advancement. Significantly, he could not see in the Talented Tenth the failure of his own program. After all, these college-trained men had succeeded by Washington's standards. They were educated and held jobs but still were subjected to Jim Crow laws and practices. Washington hoped to lift up his race through education. The members of the Talented Tenth, graduates of some of the best colleges and universities in America, including Harvard, were highly educated but remained second-class citizens who sat in Jim Crow cars and were denied access to restaurants and hotels because of their skin color. They dressed well and set good examples of citizenship. Certainly they knew how to use a toothbrush, that basic symbol of hygiene and civilization that Washington spoke of so often. If successful black professionals were subjected to Jim Crow laws, what would happen to the millions who remained trapped in agricultural jobs that were little more than slavery by another name?

While Washington engaged in an intense struggle with those who challenged his leadership, large events began to shatter his carefully constructed bargain with the white South. All his influence, public or private, could not stem the tide of worsening racial conditions in the United States. In 1906, in the progressive New South city of Atlanta, just eleven years after Washington's speech that launched his career as a race leader, the city and state were in the midst of one of the most virulent anti-black gubernatorial campaigns on record. The contest matched two longtime newspaper rivals both vying for the governorship: Hoke Smith, former publisher of the *Atlanta Journal*, and Clark Howell, editor of the *Atlanta Constitution*. Both candidates ran on a platform that disfranchised black voters and preserved white supremacy.

It was Howell who had witnessed Washington's 1895 speech and called it the beginning of a moral revolution in

America. What he meant was that Washington accepted social segregation and refused to agitate for political rights.
Howell's definition of moral revolution meant settlement of
the race issue with blacks resigned to a second-class status
that minimized their social or political activity. To men like
Smith and Howell, voting rights could lead to economic and
social equality for blacks. Howell had watched Washington's
career carefully and was the first to sound the alarm whenever Washington went beyond the formula of the Atlanta
Address. In their campaign, Howell and Smith exchanged
broadsides on the best plan to keep blacks in their place and
prevent "uppity" Negroes from gaining a foothold in the
city.

Howell in effect accused Smith of not being a strong
enough segregationist for the job. Smith turned up his rhetoric against blacks, shouting, "What does Civilization owe
the negro" Nothing! *Nothing*! NOTHING!" Hoke Smith won
the election that fall as a Progressive reformer, demonstrat-
ing how far Progressive politics in the South were from the
concerns of Georgia blacks. Smith was a Progressive and a
populist in all areas except race. He called for the regulation
of railroads, more public school funding, the creation of a
juvenile court system, and the end of the horrors of the convict-lease system, the one issue on which both candidates
agreed with Washington and Du Bois.

The strong racist language of the Georgia gubernatorial
campaign and the way Atlanta newspapers played on white
fears of black domination helped create a climate for disas-
ter. Throughout the campaign newspapers contained lurid
stories of black crime, the threat of black men raping white
women, and the need to clean up black saloons along Decatur Street, which the press called a seedbed for crime and
licentious behavior. On the evening of Saturday, September
22, 1906, a major race riot began that was not completely

ended for five days, though most of the violence occurred in the first two days. On the first day of the riot the newspapers had carried accounts of four alleged rapes of white women by black men. These were unsubstantiated rumors, but large crowds of white men and boys filled the streets that afternoon and into the evening. The crowd became a mob that marched down Decatur Street and other black sections of the city, destroying black businesses, pulling blacks from streetcars and beating them, and shooting and killing two dozen or more citizens before the riot ended. Five whites also died in the rioting, including two policemen and a woman who suffered a heart attack when she saw the mob.

The state militia took control of the city but found it difficult to stop the violence. While black citizens armed themselves and prepared to defend their property, thousands of others fled the city to safety. One young black witness to the riot, Walter White, a light-skinned, blue-eyed, thirteen-year-old, was handed a gun by his father and told to shoot any of the mob that came onto their property. White later wrote that was the night he realized he was black. He would later become the leader of the NAACP.

Booker T. Washington was horrified by the riot. He had been in Atlanta just three weeks earlier for a meeting of the National Negro Business League. His speech in Atlanta on August 30, covered by Atlanta newspapers, had contained his usual formula of promoting black economic progress and boosting the South as the best place for blacks to succeed. He was fully aware of the heightened racial climate engendered by the gubernatorial campaign, yet he addressed the issue of black crime as he often had before. "The negro is committing too much crime north and south," he said. "We should see to it, as far as our influence extends, that crimes are fewer in number; otherwise the race will permanently suffer." He condemned lynching as something that both whites and blacks were responsible to stop. He told the Business League, ". . . let us bear in mind that every man, white or black, who takes the law into his hands to lynch or burn or shoot human beings supposed to be, or guilty of crime is insulting the executive, judicial, and lawmaking bodies of the state in which he resides."

Washington saw race violence in class terms. The better classes of white people did not engage in lynching, and the better classes of black people were not criminals. Blacks "who owned homes, who are taxpayers, who have a trade or other regular occupation," and those with an education were not likely to commit crimes. Washington was trying to make a reasoned appeal to tone down Atlanta's incendiary atmosphere, but some of his remarks could easily be construed to justify violence. He did not stop after noting the better class of blacks who did not commit crime; he also felt the need to talk about those who did. "Which is the class that is guilty, as a rule, of criminal action?" he asked before answering his own question. "They are the loafers, the drunkards and gamblers, men for the main part without permanent employment, who own no homes, who have no bank account, who glide from one community to another without interest in any one spot." What Washington could never control was how the newspapers played his remarks. The *Atlanta Constitution* gave a fair account of the speech but gave the story an incendiary headline: "LAW-BREAKING NEGROES WORST MENACE TO RACE."

Shortly after the Atlanta Riot, on the evening of September 28, Washington went to the city to help restore calm. He had been in New York when the riot broke out, and his first response was an interview in the *New York World*. With the riot causing a national stir, Washington responded by urging blacks to "exercise self-control and not make the fatal mistake of attempting to retaliate." He restated his belief that the "best element of both races" needed to work together to improve conditions. While he found the riot disturbing, he tried to place it in brighter perspective by saying it was a "lesson from which all can profit." He reminded readers that while there was "disorder in one community there is peace and harmony in thousands of others." He blamed the riot on a few "despicable criminals." Many blacks, including Washington's own friend T. Thomas Fortune, thought resistance might be the only way to stop such riots and that nonresistance might result in more violence. Washington, however, preached nonviolence. Throughout his life he urged blacks not to rely on guns for protection because nine times out of ten the gun would lead to more violence and bloodshed, not less.

W. E. B. Du Bois had a different take on the Atlanta Riot. He was in rural Alabama when it broke out, and he took the next train home to Atlanta where he sat with a shotgun. Fortunately no rioters tested his will to use it. On the train back to the city he wrote a long, tangled, impassioned poem, "The Litany at Atlanta," which said in part:

> Bewildered we are, and passion-tost, mad with the madness of a mobbed and mocked and murdered people; straining at the armposts of Thy Throne, we raise our shackled hands and charge Thee, God, by the bones of our stolen fathers, by the tears of our dead mothers, by the very blood of Thy crucified Christ: *What meaneth this?* Tell us the Plan; give us the Sign! *Keep not thou silence, O God!*

A month after the riot Clark Howell, an example of the "best" whites in South, wrote to Washington, the "best" black man, to say that the racial situation "seems to be growing worse instead of better." He cited newspaper stories about rape and said these stories were provoking greater race prejudice. Howell blamed the Northern press and Northern agitators, and Washington agreed that radical papers in the North were adding to the problem. "It is a pity," Howell wrote, "that your race as a whole should be made to suffer from the offense of its brutal and criminal element and yet that is the situation." Howell complimented Washington for his good work in condemning "the Northern hot heads and incendiaries who are endeavoring to incite the Negroes of the South." Howell always tried to control Washington in the dance of the two men over racial matters.

The Atlanta Riot was not the only major blow that Washington suffered that summer and fall of 1906. Five weeks before the riot, while the Niagara Movement was in the midst of its second meeting at Harpers Ferry, complete with Washington's spies and infiltrators, far across the country in the small town of Brownsville, Texas, at the very southern tip of the state on the Mexican border, a skirmish occurred that would shake Washington's carefully constructed empire to its very foundations.

On the evening of August 13, 1906, a band of unidentified men opened fire on the streets of Brownsville near Fort Brown, where three companies of black soldiers of the Twenty-fifth Infantry regiment had been moved from their previous post in Nebraska. A bartender was killed and a policeman badly wounded. Just who was responsible for the incident was never proven. But townspeople who resented black soldiers in their midst blamed a dozen members of the black regiment for the shooting, even though the commander of the fort said all men were accounted for at the time. The twelve accused soldiers were imprisoned. The remainder of the regiment, 155 men, remained silent when asked what they knew of the incident. After several cursory investigations the entire regiment of 167 men was charged with insubordination, with the recommendation that they be dishonorably discharged.

The case went to President Theodore Roosevelt, who delayed any decision until after the November 1906 congressional elections, hoping for black support at the polls. Because officials in Brownsville and elsewhere in Texas had urged Roosevelt to remove the troops even before this incident, many observers saw the charges against the men as trumped up for the purpose of getting black troops out of Brownsville. Washington used all the persuasion in his arsenal to convince Roosevelt not to dismiss the entire regiment. His long-standing relationship with Roosevelt was on the line. No other black man had Roosevelt's ear as Washington did, but the president stubbornly refused to listen to him or be swayed by petitions from other sources urging restraint in the matter. On November 5 Roosevelt issued the order to dishonorably discharge all three companies for their conspiracy of silence and insubordination. Many career soldiers with distinguished records were thrown out of the service with no pay, no pensions, and no chance for other jobs with the government. Washington wrote to Roosevelt describing the bitter disappointment within the black community resulting from the president's decision, especially coming as it did on the heels of the Atlanta Riot. There was, Washington said, a "deep feeling that some wholly innocent men are being punished." He questioned the timing of the president's decision immediately after an election in which the Republican party had sought black votes in the South.

Emmett Scott and T. Thomas Fortune urged Washington to break off his relationship with Roosevelt because of the Brownsville decision. They took the long view: Roosevelt would be in office only two more years, and Washington needed to think of his future beyond that. Fortune wrote to Washington "as the controlling genius of the Tuskegee Institute and leader of the Afro-American people, and your future

"*BLAME THAT KNIFE ANYWAY! THAT MAKES TWICE I'VE CUT MYSELF!*"

A 1906 cartoon from the *Denver Post* depicts Theodore Roosevelt's inept handling of the "Negro question." He damaged relations with white Southerners by dining with Washington and alienated blacks when he discharged black soldiers at Brownsville, Texas.

will depend largely on how far you allow it to be understood that you are sponsor for what he says and does as far as the Afro-American people are concerned."

Washington chose to remain loyal to Roosevelt despite his considerable personal disappointment in the dismissal of the black soldiers. Instead of criticizing the president he did everything in his power to control the issue. He urged black newspapers to cease their agitation on the matter. Washington's friend and confidant Charles W. Anderson of New York warned Washington that the press, white and black, was beginning to see him as a leader of only a faction of blacks. Washington's answer was to redouble his efforts to maintain the status quo and calm the frayed nerves and aroused passions that followed from the Atlanta Riot and the Brownsville incident.

Racial conditions in America were indeed growing worse, inflamed by sensational stories, heightened competition for jobs, and increasing racial segregation. In the summer of 1908 another major race riot occurred, this time in the North, in the hometown of Abraham Lincoln, Springfield, Illinois. A mob formed to seek revenge on two black men held in jail in separate cases for the alleged crime of rape or attempted rape. One case later proved to be a complete fabrication, and the other a matter of breaking and entering that involved no rape. Nonetheless when jailers successfully spirited the prisoners away to another town, the mob turned its anger on a Jewish community and two black neighborhoods of Springfield, burning houses and businesses as blacks fled the city. The state militia was able to protect black citizens who fled to the Springfield Arsenal for protection, but the mob continued on its rampage, killing and hanging the body of one old black man because he had married a white woman thirty-two years earlier. Another black man was shot when he attempted to protect his property by firing a warning shot in the air. His body was dragged through the streets and hoisted up into a tree. Seven blacks were killed and dozens of black houses and businesses destroyed. More than 12,000 whites lined the streets to watch the fires, and members of the mob cut fire hoses so that the buildings could not be saved. In the aftermath 107 persons were indicted, but only one was convicted—of the minor crime of stealing a sword.

A few days after the Springfield Riot, Washington issued a statement on lynching from Baltimore, where he was attending a meeting of the National Negro Business League. Making no reference to the riot, he began by saying, "Within the past sixty days twenty-five Negroes have been lynched in different parts of the United States. Of this number only four were even charged with criminal assault upon women." He singled out a brutal lynching in Greenville, Texas, where a black man was doused with oil and set afire before a crowd of one thousand, including women and children. "How long can our Christian civilization stand this?" Washington asked. While he decried mob violence, he dulled his own sense of outrage lest it seem too strong, adding, "I am making no special plea for the Negro, innocent or guilty, but I am calling attention to the danger that threatens our civilization."

The Springfield Riot moved Washington to issue a plea to end lynching that was later published as a pamphlet. This was as far as he would go. Elsewhere, however, moral outrage boiled over and set in motion a series of events that would be the culmination of the Niagara Movement's efforts to protest racial injustice and a rising concern among Northern white liberals and socialist reformers that something needed to be done. Oswald Garrison Villard, a descendant of abolitionists, used the pages of the *New York Evening Post* to declare the Springfield Riot the latest example of a wave of crime and lawlessness that was sweeping the country. Other journalists pointed out that if this could happen in Lincoln's hometown, in a state that had never known slavery, it could happen anywhere. William English Walling, another young socialist reformer, writing in the liberal journal *The Independent*, called race riots an ominous sign of an ongoing race war in America.

Villard had long been a supporter of black causes, a friend of Booker T. Washington, and an advocate of the Tuskegee Idea. Washington cultivated his friendship over the years not only because of Villard's illustrious ancestors but because of his position as a powerful New York publisher. But Villard had grown tired of Washington's lack of public outrage about racial injustice and his conservative program. Like many others, white and black, Villard was pulling away from Washington's style of leadership, if not from Washington himself. Villard wrote to his uncle Francis J. Garrison in the spring of 1909 that he was growing weary with Washington's solution to race advancement. "It is always the same thing," Villard wrote, "platitudes, stories, high praise for the southern white man who is helping the negro up."

Villard saw exactly what Charles W. Anderson had warned Washington about. There were now two distinct factions of black leadership, one headed by Washington and the other by Du Bois. Washington may have believed he was still king of the hill, but power was draining away. His failure to influence Roosevelt in the Brownsville affair hurt him among blacks as well as whites who promoted racial justice. His bromides about gaining an education and striving for economic success were fine as far as they went, but they seemed totally inadequate and far too gradual to address the growing hostility and cruelty of Jim Crow practices.

As Villard moved to a more militant position and allied himself with Northern black intellectuals, Washington concluded that the editor did not understand people. He had mistakenly aligned himself with "bitter and resentful" blacks and whites who were "dreamers and otherwise impractical people, who do not understand our conditions in the South." Still, for a while at least, Villard saw himself as a bridge between the two factions. Villard, Mary White Ovington (a close friend of Du Bois's), William English Walling, and others decided to call for a national Negro conference to address the deteriorating race conditions. They would issue their appeal on the hundredth anniversary of the birth of Abraham Lincoln. The group first met at Walling's New York apartment and, as it expanded, moved its meetings to the Liberal Club in the city. Villard invited Washington to the conference, telling him candidly that he expected the gathering to be dominated by neither Washington nor Du Bois. But Washington demurred, saying that perhaps a better meeting would result if he were not present. He did not wish to appear too cozy with radical reformers, preferring to watch them from a safe distance.

The National Negro Conference met on May 31 and June 1, 1909. It included whites and blacks of both sexes—social workers, journalists, anthropologists, neo-abolitionists, liberals, socialists, radicals, and clergy—who represented a cross section of forces that closely resembled the Northern players in the Progressive Era, with a special emphasis on blacks from the Niagara Movement. The meeting revealed a more complex variety of opinions on race advancement than Washington would ever have tolerated in organizations he controlled. All was not harmonious; the firebrand Monroe Trotter objected to every resolution put forward. If there was any agreement at the conference it was that Washington's leadership was inadequate for the task. Du Bois made it clear, in a letter he wrote to the *Boston Transcript*, that Washington expected blacks to follow his lead when it came to politics. "Mr. Washington," Du Bois wrote, "has for the last eight years allowed himself to be made the sole referee for all political action concerning 10,000,000 Americans. Few appointments have been made without his consent, and others' political policies have been deferred to him." He called Washington "the political boss of the Negro race in America."

From this conference the National Association for the Advancement of Colored People was born. Washington was kept at arm's length from organizational sessions and the early meetings of the NAACP. The Niagara Movement soon merged with the NAACP and ceased to exist as a separate organization. Some Southerners could be found in the NAACP, but in its early years it was a Northern urban movement with mostly white leadership, a strong black presence, and liberal and radical elements that stood in stark contrast to

Washington's conservative leadership and the conservative business and educational organizations that were part of his network.

Washington watched the NAACP closely. His lieutenants in various cities infiltrated and spied on its meetings. In New York, where the primary action occurred during the organization's early years, Charles W. Anderson observed the NAACP and reported regularly to Washington. When the NAACP began to publish *The Crisis* under the direction of Du Bois, Washington became alarmed at this new militant publication that rose to challenge the status quo. Its circulation grew to rival Fortune's *New York Age*, Washington's chief mouthpiece in New York. Washington ordered Fortune to increase the circulation of the *Age*, to counter *The Crisis*.

Spying on the NAACP and efforts to minimize its impact had very little effect on the growth of the organization. Washington sensed, however, that its existence alone would make his life more difficult in the South, where white supremacists would look upon the new group as a pack of troublemakers and Northern agitators. On at least two occasions that can be documented, Washington hired reporters, using Charles W. Anderson as a go-between, to spread unfavorable stories about some of the NAACP's founders and their associates. As an example, in the spring of 1908 the Cosmopolitan Society of America, usually referred to as the Cosmopolitan Club, held a dinner at a New York restaurant to promote interracial understanding. The club had been founded by Mary White Ovington, who presided at the dinner. Oswald Garrison Villard was a speaker. A reporter for the *New York American* covered the dinner, and his article appeared the next day with the headline "WHITE GIRLS AT 'EQUALITY' FEAST WITH NEGROES." Through innuendo the story suggested that the white girls were much sought after by black attendees. And a subhead in the story

claimed "ORATORS OPENLY ADVOCATE THE INTERMARRIAGE
OF WHITES AND BLACKS."

On January 25, 1911, on the occasion of another Cosmopolitan Club dinner, Washington asked Anderson to see if he
could get the same reporter who covered the 1908 dinner to attend. Anderson could not find the same man, but he arranged
for lurid coverage nonetheless and sent Washington clippings
from several newspapers. The day after the dinner Anderson
wrote Washington that the event had been well handled by
the press "with proper sensational headlines of the dinner."

The account of the dinner in the *New York Press* left little to the imagination.

THREE RACES SIT
AT BANQUET FOR MIXED MARRIAGE

Fashionable White Women at
Board with Negroes, Japs
And Chinamen to Promote
Their "Cause"—Yellow and
Black Representatives Show
Most Enthusiasm

COMOPOLITAN SOCIETY
ANNOUNCES MISSION

Intermarriage of Kinky-Haired Peoples
with Caucasians Keynote of
Blow-Out at Cafe Boulevard—
Africans Have Time of Their Life,
But the Waiters Are Sorely Puzzled.

The report said, "White women, evidently of the cultured
and wealthy classes, fashionably attired in low-cut gowns
leaned over tables to chat confidentially with negro men of
the true African type." Exactly what Washington hoped to

gain by discrediting Mary White Ovington and other leaders of the NAACP with such scandalous headlines is not clear. Apparently he hoped to portray them as radicals outside the mainstream of social acceptance, as a way to smear the NAACP as too radical to be taken seriously. In Jim Crow America, even in some Northern cities, such interracial dinners would surely raise eyebrows and question motives. Washington was not above playing the race card on his enemies.

In 1911 Washington suffered a blow to his otherwise impeccable public reputation when he was assaulted, beaten, and arrested in New York City. Washington guarded closely his public image and personal reputation, believing that even the slightest hint of scandal would ruin him in the South. The New York incident is shrouded in mystery and bizarre behavior that may never be fully explained. On the evening of March 19 Washington was walking alone in the streets of New York along West Sixty-third Street, not far from the notorious Tenderloin district, known for its dives and prostitution. He had spoken that afternoon at the Mount Olivet Baptist Church and at the Church of the Pilgrims, both in Brooklyn. He returned to his midtown Manhattan hotel but then left and took the subway to his destination. That night, he would later say, he went looking for Daniel Smith, Tuskegee's auditor, and ended up in a vestibule checking the addresses on mailboxes. He rang one doorbell several times with no answer, walked into the street, and returned twice more to ring the bell. At one point a white woman passed him and reported to her husband that Washington had looked at her and said, "Hello, sweetheart." Her husband, Henry A. Ulrich, a dog kennel operator, challenged Washington, asked him what he was doing, and proceeded to beat him about the head. Washington fled into the street. A passerby handed Ulrich a cane so he could continue to beat Washington. With Ulrich still swinging the cane at him, Washington made his

way to a plainclothes policeman standing on a nearby corner. He fell on his hands and knees before the officer, bleeding badly. Ulrich told the cop he was chasing a thief.

At the station house Washington convinced the police of
his identity, and he was released. Ulrich was charged with
assault. Washington went to the hospital, where he received
sixteen stitches in his head. His ear was torn, and he had facial bruises. His lawyer said he was too ill to make an early
court appearance. The press covered the story in a sensational manner. How could the most famous black person
in America, the distinguished Southern educator, wind up
being beaten—in the Tenderloin district, of all places? Emmett Scott tried to control press coverage and find a plausible
explanation for Washington's actions that night. One story
said he had been mistaken for a kidnapper. With Washington's reputation on the line, Scott arranged for testimonials
from President William Howard Taft and other prominent
citizens. Taft wrote a glowing endorsement of Washington
and his work, adding, "It would be the nation's loss if this
untoward incident in any way impaired your great power for
good in the solution of one of the most difficult problems
before us." The president said he would stand by him.

The Ulrich affair dragged on in the newspapers, which
included pictures of Washington with his head in bandages
beneath his derby. Many unsubstantiated elements of the
story remained. Washington could not explain why he was
looking for Tuskegee's auditor at an address in New York
when the auditor lived in New Jersey. When Daniel Smith
talked to the press he said he did not know of a meeting with
Washington, and whenever they did meet it was always at
Smith's office. Washington denied being drunk, something
he had never before had to do. He went on to say he had
never been drunk in his life—which may have been true,
but there is no doubt that Washington liked Scotch, which

he received by the case from his friend Charles Anderson each Christmas. In the end Washington expected the public to take his word that he was doing nothing wrong that night. He, his lawyer, and Scott considered negotiations with Ulrich and his wife, using an undercover agent, to get them to change their stories. Washington desperately wanted Ulrich to say he was doing nothing improper that night.

At Ulrich's trial, eight months later, a three-member panel of judges listened to the testimony and then spent five minutes in deliberation before acquitting Ulrich of all charges. Washington stuck to his story of trying to find the Tuskegee auditor, but his responses were vague and inconclusive. Before Ulrich could leave the court building he was arrested on another charge of deserting his family and children in New Jersey, though this was little consolation for Washington. The incident fell from public view, but in the South white supremacists continued to raise doubts about Washington's behavior that night. The racist novelist Thomas Dixon charged there was a lie in there someplace, either on Ulrich's part or Washington's. Most of Washington's enemies among blacks gave him the benefit of the doubt. Even Monroe Trotter refused to attack him when he was down. The NAACP passed a sympathy resolution for the beating Washington took, but it stopped short of giving him a vote of confidence like the one President Taft had sent.

Physically Washington was wearing out. He was fifty-five years old at the time of the Ulrich beating. Just before that unfortunate incident he had been at the famous health sanitorium in Battle Creek, Michigan, run by John Harvey Kellogg. All his life he had thrown himself completely into work, seldom stopping for a vacation. The few times he did relax were on several ocean voyages to Europe, where he would often sleep for long periods of time while aboard ship. But by 1911 it was clear that the years had begun to take a toll on him. His light eyes had always shown prominently in photographs taken earlier in his career. Photographs taken near the end of his life show him aging rapidly, with tired eyes and sunken facial features.

Woodrow Wilson's inauguration in 1913 spelled the end of Washington's White House influence. His time as an adviser to Republican presidents was over, as was his ability to control patronage for black officeholders. Wilson, a Virginian by birth, the former president of Princeton University and governor of New Jersey, had spent most of his formative years in Augusta, Georgia. A Southerner to the core, he brought a new level of Jim Crow to the nation's capital. He fired most of the black appointees, including the current minister to Haiti, a traditionally black appointment, and replaced black officeholders with whites. Black employees in the Post Office and Treasury departments were segregated and given separate restrooms and dining facilities. W. E. B. Du Bois complained from the pages of *The Crisis*: "The federal government has set the colored apart as if mere contact with them were contamination. Behind screens and closed doors they now sit as though leprous. How long will it be before the hateful epithets of 'Nigger' and 'Jim Crow' are openly applied?"

Washington's national leadership was further eroded by the rise of a new black militancy as exemplified in the NAACP. No single leader arose to take his place as the most prominent and well-known black man in America. Instead the torch was passed unceremoniously to institutions and institutional players, and to the vigor of new ideas. Du Bois never enjoyed a charisma among the masses of blacks and whites that Booker T. Washington did. Washington remained personally popular even while his ideas and his strategy for the advancement of his race became outmoded. He worked diligently and tirelessly until the very end of his life. In late

Washington in Jacksonville, Florida, 1912. *(Library of Congress)*

October 1915 he wrote to his wife that he had spoken to two large meetings at Yale "and felt no bad effects." He had been ill but was continuing his rigorous schedule. But a few days later he was in a New York hospital in serious condition with kidney failure, hardening of the arteries, and high blood pressure. When stories of his hospitalization appeared in the press, some said he had had a nervous breakdown. One doctor made a vague reference to diseases related to his race, leading to speculation that Washington had a venereal disease, which was false.

The last major item Washington addressed before he died was an exchange between him and Emmett Scott about their response to the new motion picture *The Birth of a Nation*. Twentieth-century technology had produced a powerful new medium for shaping minds, one Washington lived to see but not to utilize. *The Birth of a Nation*, a silent film, was the first full-length feature motion picture ever made. Directed by D. W. Griffith, one of the early masters and innovators of the movies, it was the most extensive, stunning, and dramatic film audiences had ever seen, and the most successful motion picture in Hollywood's first two decades. It told a sweeping, panoramic story of the Civil War and Reconstruction based on a racist novel, *The Clansman*, written by one of Washington's longtime critics, Thomas Dixon, a former Johns Hopkins classmate and friend of President Woodrow Wilson. At a special screening of the film at the White House, Wilson supposedly remarked that it was "like writing history with lightning." Whether he said this or not, the producer used quotations from Wilson's book *A History of the American People* in the film to give it the appearance of a presidential endorsement and to promote its historical accuracy. Audiences believed the film was a true depiction of American history.

While the film portrayed the South and the Confederacy in a romantic and sympathetic manner, the raw emotion and most blatant racial stereotyping in the film takes place in scenes dealing with Reconstruction, where the Ku Klux Klan heroically rises to save the South from Negro domination. Radical Republican Thaddeus Stevens, champion of black rights during Reconstruction—called Stoneman in the film— is portrayed as a tool of his mulatto mistress who uses Stevens's power in the House of Representatives in her schemes for black domination. Black characters in the film fall into several stereotypical categories. Most slaves are loyal to their white masters, just as Booker T. Washington described them in his Atlanta Address in 1895, when he urged whites to cast their bucket down "among the eight millions of Negroes whose habits you know, whose fidelity and love you have tested in days when to have proved treacherous meant the ruin of your firesides." In the Reconstruction scenes of the film, black characters take on sinister qualities as inexperienced, unqualified participants in Southern politics, hellbent on racial domination of the South.

In his Atlanta Address twenty years earlier, Washington had referred to the period of black participation in Reconstruction politics when he said, "Ignorant and inexperienced, it is not strange that in the first years of our new life we began at the top instead of at the bottom; that a seat in Congress or the state legislature was more sought than real estate or industrial skill; that the political convention or stump speaking had more attractions than starting a dairy farm or a truck garden." This was the same premise used in *The Birth of a Nation*. Washington's expedient acceptance of the Southern view of Reconstruction history two decades earlier was now thrown back in his face in stark racist terms. Several prominent black characters in *The Birth of a Nation* seem motivated solely by their desire to marry white women. In the climactic scene a sinister black man, Gus, stalks Flora, one of the young white heroines of the film. To escape her pursuer, she jumps from a cliff to her death. The Ku Klux Klan avenges the death of this fair maiden by capturing Gus and lynching him.

Just two weeks before he died and while he was in the hospital in New York, Washington received a letter from Scott with a clipping of a story in the *Atlanta Constitution* that could not but add to Washington's woes. *The Birth of a Nation* was beginning to appear in theaters in the South. In Houston, Scott reported, as white audiences witnessed the scene in which a black man pursues a white girl, men leaped from their seats and shouted, "Lynch him! Lynch him!"

The clipping from the *Constitution* assured Atlantans that a citizens group, hoping to ban the showing of the film in Atlanta, would be denied and that the film was not fueling race prejudice. Instead the *Constitution* called it "a great triumph of scenic art." The NAACP led efforts to ban the film because it incited strong emotions and even riots, but the controversy over a possible ban only added to the publicity the film received.

In so many ways *The Birth of a Nation* symbolized the utter failure of Washington's strategy of conciliation. His acceptance of the white Southern view of Reconstruction politics, with the bottom rung inappropriately on top, now came back to haunt him. Where he had used the idea to win over whites in his Atlanta Address, twenty years later the same concept was used powerfully in a motion picture to justify the terrorism of the original Klan of the 1860s and 1870s. Racial prejudice in Jim Crow America had reached the point where it could be enjoyed as entertainment and history. Washington and Scott worked to find a filmmaker who could tell a positive story about racial advancement. Scott continued this effort after Washington's death, and in 1918 *The Birth of a Race* delivered a different message. But it never competed successfully with *The Birth of a Nation*. Just two weeks after Washington's death, on Thanksgiving, inspired by the powerful racism of the film, a band of hooded men gathered on Stone Mountain just outside Atlanta, not far from where Washington had delivered his Atlanta Address, and the Ku Klux Klan was born again.

Washington preferred to die at home, so he decided to make the arduous train trip from New York to Tuskegee. Accompanied by his wife, he arrived at Tuskegee at midnight on November 13, 1915. Washington died at his home, The Oaks, on his beloved campus in the Black Belt of Alabama, four hours and forty-five minutes later.

Eulogies and editorials filled the nation's newspapers. W. E. B. Du Bois wrote in the pages of the *The Crisis*: "The death of Mr. Washington marks an epoch in the history of America. He was the greatest Negro leader since Frederick Douglass, and the most distinguished man, white or black, to come out of the South since the Civil War." Du Bois could not stop there. "On the other hand, in stern justice, we must lay on the soul of this man, a heavy responsibility for the consummation of Negro disfranchisement, the decline of the Negro college and public school and the firmer establishment of color caste in this land."

This final, harsh verdict from Du Bois is certainly understandable given their rivalry and history together, and the continued growth of the Jim Crow menace throughout the period of Washington's leadership. But is it fair? Can one man, even a leader, be responsible for the fate of an entire race of ten million people? Washington's life story shows how success may be achieved with self-help and determination. Education was his salvation: through it he gained personal freedom and international fame. He built his entire program for race advancement on what had worked for him. Education remains the most powerful force for freedom. But Washington underestimated how far education and economic advancement could take black Americans without political rights, the other major source of freedom. The white politicians of his time in the South knew that taking away the vote would stifle black advancement.

Washington's Atlanta Compromise in 1895 gave away too much. It never bought him the time he needed for his program of education and economic gain to take root. He hoped that rising political and social hostility toward his race during Reconstruction and the rise of Jim Crow could be overcome through bargaining with the white majority, seeking common ground, and avoiding protest that he believed would

only increase violence against blacks. It is impossible, however, to imagine economic gain without political rights. This
is not a judgment of hindsight; Washington's contemporaries
were leery of his compromise from the beginning. Washington himself knew that political agitation, generations of it,
ultimately ended slavery. Yet he consciously avoided protest
and sought peace by seeking the cooperation of the white
race. There had been enough violence in his lifetime; he tried
to find a peaceful settlement. He sought an end to the undeclared race war that continued in America for generations
after the Civil War ended. This was no longer a battle that
saw armies fighting in the field, but it was a war nonetheless
to reenslave blacks and return the South to its antebellum
ways where possible. Washington underestimated just how
extensively this new war was fought in the political arena,
not in the realms of economics or education.

Frederick Douglass's thundering moral outrage was not
Washington's style. He tried something different. He led a
moral Christian life, turned the other cheek to his white
detractors, and countered prejudice by his example of good
citizenship and public optimism. As an American celebrity
of great substance, Washington, the one black man everyone knew, thought his personal example would assuage
race prejudice. His personal popularity was immense and
no doubt influenced many Americans, black and white, in
a positive manner—but never enough to stem the tide of
growing racism, disfranchisement, and segregation. He adhered to the idea that the race problem of his time had to be
solved in the South, where the majority of blacks lived. In
his Atlanta Address he sought primarily to reach Southern
whites, more than any other group, with his message. He
succeeded beyond his wildest dreams. The South, and the
entire nation, was eager to embrace a plan that offered an
opportunity for racial peace.

What Washington saw as a compromise, white Southerners took to mean capitulation. Blacks would stay in their place, under Washington's plan, just as white politicians demanded. White newspaper editors never permitted him to stray from the Atlanta Compromise without admonition. They kept him on a short leash of his own making.

The Jim Crow Era continued the undeclared race war that began the minute slaves were freed. One man, one idea, one compromise was not enough to stop this war. The ideas of W. E. B. Du Bois added the missing dimension to Washington's program—agitation for civil rights and standing up to Jim Crow, not bargaining with it. But even with the new urgency and the new ideas of Du Bois and his allies, it would take another half-century to overcome the worst aspects of Jim Crow. It did not occur completely even in the lifetime of Du Bois, who lived another forty-eight years after Washington died. In this context, and with this hindsight, it would seem that Du Bois's judgment that Washington was responsible for the worsening of race conditions in America places too much of a burden on one man who did so much to help so many up from slavery.

Neither Washington nor Du Bois was ever free of Jim Crow strictures. Neither man chose the times in which he lived. Du Bois wrote in *The Souls of Black Folk*, "One ever feels his two-ness, — an American, a Negro; two souls, two thoughts, two unreconciled strivings; two warring ideals in one dark body. . . ." Both he and Washington wanted nothing more than to be accepted as Americans. But deep-seated racism constructed during centuries of slavery and unleashed in new but equally virulent forms during Reconstruction and well into the twentieth century demanded that their talents and their lives be used up in the struggle against Jim Crow. They were black leaders, but they were also American leaders who sought to expand the definition of democracy.

A Note on Sources

THE BEST full-length biography of Booker T. Washington is the two-volume work of Louis R. Harlan, *Booker T. Washington: The Making of a Black Leader, 1856–1901* (New York, 1972) and *Booker T. Washington: The Wizard of Tuskegee, 1901–1915* (New York, 1983), which was indispensable in the writing of this book. The best of Harlan's many essays on Washington, originally published in various scholarly journals, may be found in Raymond W. Smock, ed., *Booker T. Washington in Perspective: Essays of Louis R. Harlan* (Jackson, Miss., 1988). This volume includes several articles that were essential in telling the story of Washington's secret life and of his dogged pursuit of one of his critics, J. Max Barber, editor of the *Voice of the Negro.*

Readers may explore Washington's private correspondence, his speeches, newspaper and magazine articles, and other documents related to his career in Louis R. Harlan and Raymond W. Smock, eds., *The Booker T. Washington Papers* (Urbana, 1972–1988), a fourteen-volume edition based on research in hundreds of archives but especially the main collection of Washington's papers at the Library of Congress. It is an essential, widely used resource on Washington's life and career. Quotations from letters, speeches, and other primary sources in this book were taken from this series. Readers may access *The Booker T. Washington Papers* online thanks to a partnership of the History Cooperative and the University of Illinois Press. The address of this website is http://www. historycooperative.org/btw/.

Booker T. Washington's two autobiographies, *The Story of My Life and Work* (Naperville [Chicago], 1900) and the far more widely read *Up from Slavery* (New York, 1901), are excellent sources of information on his early life and his career as an educator and builder of Tuskegee Institute. There is very little documentation on his childhood and youth, so these autobiographies are essential resources. Both autobiographies and selections from other Washington autobiographical writing may be found in Volume 1 of the *Booker T. Washington Papers* and at the History Cooperative website mentioned above.

Washington prepared an anecdotal volume, *My Larger Education* (New York, 1911), designed as a sequel to *Up from Slavery*. It was largely ghostwritten and is less useful, but it does contain some of Washington's reflections on his relationship with the press, his friendship with Theodore Roosevelt, and his feelings about his critics—all written, however, for public consumption, so the observations lack a critical tone. While Washington was living, work began on another review of his career, but it was not completed until after his death: Emmett J. Scott and Lyman Beecher Stowe, *Booker T. Washington: Builder of a Civilization* (1916). This is interesting as one of the last examples of the positive image-making of Washington's and Scott's Tuskegee Machine designed to showcase Washington's accomplishments in light of his critics, black and white.

Another invaluable study used throughout this book is August Meier, *Negro Thought in America, 1880–1915: Racial Ideologies in the Age of Booker T. Washington* (Ann Arbor, 1963). It remains the best single resource for understanding the conflicting intellectual currents among blacks, including an excellent analysis of Washington's ideology as well as those of his critics in the Talented Tenth, especially W. E. B. Du Bois. Michael Rudolph West, *The Education of Booker T. Washington* (New York, 2006) is an outstanding contribution to understanding Washington's efforts to develop a race-relations framework to confront Jim Crow. West's idea that Washington's race strategy developed early in his life, largely at Hampton, led me to explore even earlier elements of his program that could be gleaned from childhood and his mastery of Webster's blue-back speller—a mainstay of middle-class values. I learned the history of the blue-back speller from E. Jennifer Monaghan, *A Common Heritage: Noah Webster's Blue-Back Speller* (Hamden, Conn., 1983).

The best study of Reconstruction is Eric Foner, *Reconstruction* (New York, 1988), though earlier works were helpful on this topic, including John Hope Franklin, *Reconstruction After the Civil War*

(Chicago, 1961) and Kenneth Stampp, The *Era of Reconstruction* (New York, 1965). An older work, Rayford Logan, *The Negro in American Life and Thought: The Nadir, 1877–1901* (New York, 1954), later reissued with the title *The Betrayal of the Negro* (New York, 1965), is still valuable for its insights into the worsening conditions faced by blacks after Reconstruction and into the time of Washington's leadership.

Any discussion of the origins of the Jim Crow system begins with C. Vann Woodward, *The Strange Career of Jim Crow* (1955). A good overview of the subject is Jerrold M. Packard, *American Nightmare: The History of Jim Crow* (2002). Attitudes of black activists during the 1960s may be found in Stokely Carmichael and Charles V. Hamilton, *Black Power: The Politics of Liberation in America* (New York, 1967). Emma Lou Thornbrough, ed., *Booker T. Washington* (Englewood Cliffs, N.J., 1969) collects impressions of Washington by his contemporaries and by scholars up to the 1960s. Differing views of Washington and his legacy at the opening of the twenty-first century may be found in Rebecca Carroll, ed., *Uncle Tom or New Negro?* (2006); this volume also contains the full text of Washington's *Up from Slavery*.

The best source for conservative black thinkers who have rediscovered Washington and are promoting his program as being of value today may be found on the website of the New Coalition for Economic and Social Change: http://www.newcoalition.org/. This organization held a symposium on Booker T. Washington in 2006. As this book was going to the press, an important new biography of Washington was published, Robert J. Norrell, *Up from History* (Cambridge, Mass., 2009). The author is critical of earlier works on Washington, especially the writings of C. Vann Woodward and Louis R. Harlan. Shelby Steele, *A Bound Man* (New York, 2008), explores types of black leadership through history and concludes that the two main categories are those who challenge the existing system and those who bargain with it. I found his analysis quite useful in this work, where I see Washington as a bargainer in public and a challenger in private.

Other works that informed this study include biographies and writings of key persons mentioned in the story, including David Levering Lewis's masterful and definitive *W. E. B. Du Bois: Biography of Race* (New York, 1993) and Lewis's comprehensive edition of Du Bois's writings, *W. E. B. Du Bois: A Reader* (New York,

1995); Manning Marable, *W. E. B. Du Bois* (Boston, 1986); Herbert Aptheker, ed., *The Correspondence of W. E. B. Du Bois: Volume I* (Amherst, Mass., 1973); Emma Lou Thornbrough, *T. Thomas Fortune* (Chicago, 1972); Frederick Douglass, *The Life and Times of Frederick Douglass* (1892 ed., reprinted New York, 1962); Benjamin Quarles, ed., *Frederick Douglass* (Englewood Cliffs, N.J., 1968); and Stephen R. Fox, *The Guardian of Boston: William Monroe Trotter* (New York, 1970). In addition to the works on Du Bois already cited, I found two additional works useful on the Washington/Du Bois issue: Jacqueline M. Moore, *Booker T. Washington, W. E. B. Du Bois, and the Struggle for Racial Uplift* (Lanham, Md., 2003) and one that first introduced me to Washington and Du Bois when I was a student, Hugh Hawkins, ed., *Booker T. Washington and His Critics* (Boston, 1962). The first journalist to explore the Washington/Du Bois controversy in terms of political factions was Ray Stannard Baker, *Following the Color Line* (1908, reprinted New York, 1964). Baker's study remains a classic for its insights on race conditions at the opening of the twentieth century.

Studies of education in the South that provide the context of Washington's era include Louis R. Harlan, *Separate and Unequal* (reprinted New York, 1968) and the best study to date, James D. Anderson, *The Education of Blacks in the South* (Chapel Hill, 1988). Anderson argues convincingly that industrial education was a major departure, even a subversion, of the freedmen's idea of universal education that fostered emancipation.

The best biography of Andrew Carnegie is David Nasaw, *Andrew Carnegie* (New York, 2006). Readers who wish to explore Carnegie's Gospel of Wealth idea should see David Nasaw, ed., *Andrew Carnegie: The "Gospel of Wealth" Essays and Other Writings* (New York, 2006). The best study of Social Darwinism is Richard Hofstadter, *Social Darwinism in American Thought* (Philadelphia, 1944; reprinted Boston, 2006).

The rise of the NAACP, including its early relations with Booker T. Washington, is well told by Charles Flint Kellogg, *NAACP* (Baltimore, 1967). Pete Daniel, *The Shadow of Slavery* (Urbana, 1972) is the best study of peonage in the South and contains an excellent account of Washington's secret involvement in the Alonzo Bailey case.

Index

Note: The following abbreviations are used in the index: BTW (Booker T. Washington); NAACP (National Association for the Advancement of Colored People; NNBL (National Negro Business League); NYC (New York City). Italicized page numbers refer to illustrations.

A NOTE ON THE AUTHOR

Raymond W. Smock was born in Jeffersonville, Indiana, and grew up in Harvey, Illinois. He studied at Roosevelt University in Chicago and at the University of Maryland, where he received a Ph.D. in American history. With Louis R. Harlan, he co-edited the fourteen-volume *Booker T. Washington Papers*. As a public historian Mr. Smock served as the first official Historian of the U.S. House of Representatives, as historical consultant to the National Constitution Center in Philadelphia, and as senior historical consultant to the twenty-six-part Public Television series *A Biography of America*. He is now director of the Robert C. Byrd Center for Legislative Studies at Shepherd University in West Virginia. He lives in Martinsburg with his wife, Phyllis.